MW01633686

THE TUDOR TREASURY

ELIZABETH NORTON

SEVENOAKS

THIS IS A SEVENOAKS BOOK

This edition published in 2015 by Sevenoaks
An imprint of the Carlton Publishing Group
20 Mortimer Street
London W1T 3JW

10 9 8 7 6 5 4 3 2 1

First published in 2014 by André Deutsch Limited

A catalogue record for this book is available from the British Library

ISBN 978 1 781 77409 0

Printed in Dubai

CONTENTS

INTRODUCTION

On 22 August 1485, a king's crown was discovered lying under a hawthorn bush not far from Market Bosworth. Lord Stanley, who had witnessed the day's events, picked his way through the bodies and debris strewn on the field to retrieve the crown. He brought it to his stepson, the victorious Henry Tudor, and placed it on his head. On that day Henry VII became king and the Tudor dynasty was born.

Three generations of Tudors would rule England for nearly 120 years, dying with Henry VII's granddaughter, Elizabeth I, in March 1603. The period and the dynasty have caught people's imaginations like no other time in British history. Partly, this is due to the personalities of the monarchs themselves. For almost the first time in English history, the reigning sovereigns can be seen in the records as people, as well as kings. The Tudor dynasty provided the miserly and cunning Henry VII, and his son, the much-married Henry VIII. The boy king, Edward VI, attempted to disinherit his two half-sisters in favour of Lady Jane Grey. She ultimately died on the block, with the Catholic Mary I reigning in her place. "Bloody" Mary failed to bear her longed-for heir, unwillingly leaving her crown to her half-sister, Elizabeth I. She was the final Tudor monarch and took England into a new age of discovery and innovation, dying unmarried and childless in 1603.

The splendour of the age cannot be attributed just to the monarchs. The people who attended their courts and who lived in the country did remarkable things. Henry VII's court was frequented by the great Erasmus, as well as the learned Sir Thomas More. Henry VIII relied on the advice of Cardinal Wolsey – the son of an Ipswich butcher – and Thomas Cromwell – a Putney blacksmith's child. Both implemented far-reaching policies in relation to religion and the government of

England. The age saw important additions to the worlds of poetry and literature, with William Shakespeare and his contemporaries bringing the theatre to the masses. At the same time, the flushing toilet was invented and given the seal of approval by Elizabeth I.

Above all, the 16th century was a time of discovery. The Americas, which had only been "discovered" by Europeans in 1492, drew much attention. At the same time, English piracy, which was aimed at Spanish treasure ships returning from the New World, was one of the direct causes of the Spanish Armada.

In 1485 Henry VII inherited a country that had been ravaged by decades of civil war, as the rival Houses of Lancaster and York battled for the throne. The first Tudor king was able to secure international recognition of his dynasty with the marriage of his son to the daughter of Ferdinand and Isabella of Spain. Henry VIII further increased England's standing on the world stage, twice personally invading France in an attempt to recapture the glory of his illustrious predecessor, Henry V, who had actually conquered the kingdom. Mary I lost the last continental English possession – Calais – when she involved herself in her husband's wars. However Elizabeth I, through diplomacy and strategic marriage negotiations, ensured that her kingdom became a major European power. Her intervention on behalf of the Protestants in the Netherlands was decisive, as was the victory over the Spanish Armada – which threatened England's independence – in 1588.

The Tudor period in England marks the beginning of the early modern period, distinguishing it from the Middle Ages. For ordinary people, life changed under the Tudors in a way that it had not done before. The 16th century was a time of great religious and scholarly reform – with new philosophies being introduced to sweep away the certainty of earlier years. With religious changes, advances in technology and the introduction of exotic foodstuffs from the New World, life for people in Tudor England was filled with new experiences and ideas.

The Tudor dynasty began with a victory in battle and ended when the last of the dynasty died peacefully in her bed. The Tudors – and the people and country over whom they ruled – fascinate us. But what were they really like?

1

THE ORIGINS OF A DYNASTY

Until 1485 all kings of England were descended in the male line from Henry II, the first king of the Plantagenet dynasty. Henry VII, who came to the throne in 1485, was different. His claim was through his Plantagenet mother, Margaret Beaufort (1443–1509), rather than through his father, Edmund, who hailed from Welsh stock. It was the marriage of Henry's grandfather, Owen Tudor (1400–1461), to Queen Catherine of Valois (1401–1437) which placed the Tudors on the path to the throne.

FALLING INTO THE QUEEN'S LAP

King Henry V of England died of dysentery in 1422, leaving a nine-month-old baby as his heir. The queen mother, Catherine of Valois, who was only 20 when she was widowed, was given no role in the regency nor even named as guardian of her son. She did, however, retain contact with her baby, carrying him into Parliament on her lap in November 1423 when the young king "shrieked and cried and sprang" according to reports.

Within a few years of Henry V's death, Catherine became romantically involved with his cousin, Edmund Beaufort (1406–1455). The idea that the dowager queen might remarry alarmed the king's minority council, with Parliament passing a statute forbidding anyone from marrying Catherine without the king's express permission – on pain of forfeiture of his lands and property. Since Henry VI was a minor and could not actually give his consent, this effectively banned the queen from marrying without danger to her husband. It certainly caused Edmund Beaufort to look elsewhere for a bride.

One man was, however, prepared to risk the statute. Catherine's household included Owen Tudor, a young Welshman who, although distantly related to noble blood, was far beneath her socially. His exact role is not recorded. He may have been the keeper of her household or of her wardrobe, both ranks far below that of the queen.

Owen was handsome and first came to Catherine's attention when, dancing vigorously at an entertainment, he stumbled and fell into her lap. This piqued the queen's interest and she began to look for him about the household. She particularly admired the athletic young man when she covertly watched him swimming, disguising herself as one of her maids so that she could meet with him secretly. When Owen tried to kiss the pretty young "maid", she struggled, scratching her cheek as she escaped. It was this that caused Owen to recognize the queen the next day. By around 1428 or 1429, the couple had married in secret.

The couple kept their relationship a secret, producing four children in quick succession: Edmund, Jasper, Owen and a daughter who died in infancy. The couple must have known that it was only a matter of time until they were exposed, but they maintained their secrecy for some years. They were only discovered in late summer 1436 when Henry VI's governors sent Catherine under restraint to Bermondsey Abbey. She died there on 3 January 1437. Her husband was imprisoned at Newgate for daring to take the king's mother as his wife.

Henry VI, who had few relatives, forged a close bond with his step-father and half-brothers, bringing them all to court when he was old enough to do so. He created his eldest half-brother, Edmund (c.1430–1456), Earl of Richmond, while the second brother, Jasper (c.1431–1495), became Earl of Pembroke. He was so fond of his brothers that he took steps to bring Edmund into the line of succession by providing him with a royal bride.

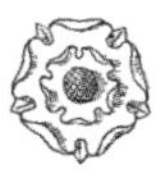

A HOLY TUDOR

While Edmund and Jasper Tudor made names for themselves at court, their brother, Owen, decided to enter the church as a monk. The younger Owen Tudor, who lived at Westminster, remained on good terms with his family, receiving payments from his nephew, King Henry VII, to meet some of his expenses. He was the last surviving child of Catherine of Valois and the senior Owen Tudor, dying in old age late in his nephew's reign.

DIVINE INTERVENTION

In 1453 the nine-year-old Margaret Beaufort (1443–1509) was the most important heiress in England. Her father was the deceased Duke of Somerset who, rumour claimed, had committed suicide when he lost royal favour. Somerset was a distant cousin of the king, Henry VI, who had few close relatives. In the early 1450s the king was showing no signs of fathering an heir of his own with his wife, Margaret of Anjou. As a result, the Beaufort branch of the family had a strong claim to the throne in the event that Henry was childless.

When Margaret Beaufort's father died, the king had granted her wardship – which gave control of her marriage and lands – to his most favoured councillor, William de la Pole, Earl of Suffolk (1396–1450). In late January or early February 1450 Suffolk, in an attempt to ensure that Margaret's wealth remained with his family, married his six-year-old ward to his eight-year-old son, John. The two children never lived together and an unconsummated childhood marriage was voidable, although Suffolk did go to the trouble of securing a dispensation from the pope for the match. Margaret's new father-in-law did not survive the marriage for long. After receiving a sentence of banishment from England, his ship was ambushed by pirates in May 1450 who beheaded him with a rusty sword.

On 23 April 1453 Margaret and her mother were ordered to attend the St George's Day celebrations at court. She obviously pleased the king since, only a few weeks later, hemade her a grant of 100 marks to spend on clothes. At the same time, he also granted her wardship to his half-brothers, Edmund and Jasper Tudor.

Margaret later told her friend, Bishop John Fisher, that she was given a choice of whether to continue with her marriage to John de la Pole or to marry the 22-year-old Edmund Tudor. Unsure what to do, she asked an old gentlewoman "whom she much loved and trusted", who advised her to ask for help from St Nicholas, the patron of maidens, "to beseech him to put in her mind what she was best to do". She began to pray to the saint for guidance.

The night before she had to make her choice, Margaret prayed especially fervently, before retiring to bed. In the sermon he wrote for her funeral, Bishop John Fisher reported that she continued to beseech the saint while lying in bed and, as she herself later admitted "whether sleeping or waking she could not assure", she had a vision. At four o'clock in the morning a man appeared to her, dressed as a bishop who, "naming unto her Edmund", bade her take him as her husband.

The next day Margaret did as she was bid, believing throughout her life that her marriage to Edmund Tudor was divinely inspired. After her earlier unconsummated marriage to John de la Pole was annulled, she married Edmund in November 1455 when she was 12. Only one year later, on 1 November 1455, Edmund died suddenly of the plague. He had assured his dynasty, however, and, at Pembroke Castle on 28 January 1457 the 13-year-old Margaret gave birth to a son. She named him Henry after his royal uncle, the king.

HENRY TUDOR'S CLAIM TO THE THRONE

Although descended from the Welsh nobility on his father's side, it was through his mother that Henry Tudor owed his claim to the throne.

The first Lancastrian king, Henry IV, seized the throne from his cousin, Richard II, in 1399 – an event that sparked the 15th-century Wars of the Roses. Henry was the son of John of Gaunt, the third surviving son of Edward III. The childless Richard II was the only surviving child of Edward's eldest son.

Henry IV's father, John of Gaunt, had only one son from his first two marriages: Henry himself. While he was still married to his second wife, he began a long-lasting affair with Katherine Swynford, a woman employed in his household. She bore him several children, who were surnamed Beaufort and who were legitimized by both the pope and by Parliament following their parents' very belated marriage in 1396. All the Beauforts were adults at the time of their parents' marriage, but they were treated well by their half-brother, Henry IV. He was not, however, prepared to pass the throne to them, inserting a caveat into the statute that legitimized them barring them from the throne.

Henry IV had four sons, so the succession prospects of the Beauforts seemed remote. This had all changed by the 1450s. Only Henry's eldest son, Henry V, produced an heir – Henry VI. Although Henry VI did eventually produce his own son, Edward of Lancaster, the lack of Lancastrian sons meant that the Beauforts were, potentially, very important. Margaret Beaufort, Henry VII's mother, was the only child of the senior Beaufort heir, John Beaufort, Duke of Somerset.

There were two rival families vying for the throne in the late 15th century. The Lancastrians were descended from the third son of Edward III, while their rivals of the house of York were descended from the second and fourth sons. The decision by Richard, Duke of York, to claim the throne in the 1450s led to the Wars of the Roses. In 1461 his son, Edward, was declared king as Edward IV, while Henry VI and his family fled. After a brief restoration of Lancastrian power between 1470 and 1471, Henry VI was murdered and his son killed in battle. This meant that Henry Tudor, who had fled to Brittany, became the heir to the House of Lancaster.

THE TUDOR NAME

The surname "Tudor" comes from the Welsh first name Tudur or Tewder. In medieval Wales, sons took their father's name as a surname. So, for example, Llewelyn, son of Owain, would become Llewelyn ap Owain. It was Owen Tudor – the husband of Catherine of Valois – who first fixed the family name as Tudor. He was actually the son of Maredudd, who had been the son of Tudur. If Owen had decided to follow tradition more closely, the dynasty could have been Maredudd rather than Tudor.

TUDOR PROPAGANDA

The last Yorkist king, Richard III (1452–1485), died fighting Henry Tudor in battle. For centuries controversy has raged over Richard and his character. Was he really the monster depicted in 15th- and 16th-century sources or a victim of Tudor propaganda?

Richard's elder brother, Edward IV, died suddenly in April 1483, leaving the throne to his 12-year-old son, Edward V (1470–1483). Within weeks of Edward IV's death, his marriage to Elizabeth Woodville (1437–1492) was declared invalid and his children thus illegitimate, and his younger brother, Richard, was declared king in Edward V's place. The deposed king and his younger brother, Richard, Duke of York (1473–1483), disappeared into the Tower of London, where they became the famous "princes in the Tower".

William Shakespeare famously depicted Richard III as a murderous hunchback, while in his history of the reign, Thomas More characterized the king in a similar manner. More considered that he was responsible for the murders of his two nephews, who were not seen alive after the summer of 1483. Most contemporaries do seem to believe that the princes were dead by late 1483, as can be seen from the fact that their mother, Edward IV's widow Queen Elizabeth Woodville, transferred her support to Henry Tudor, providing that he married her daughter. That the princes were murdered by Richard is the most likely explanation, although Henry Tudor and, implausibly, even his mother, Margaret Beaufort, have been suggested as possible murderers.

Many of the excesses of the Tudor depictions of Richard can be dismissed. The claim in John Rous's *Historia Regum*, which appeared soon after Richard's death, that the "tyrant" remained in his mother's womb for two years before "issuing forth with teeth and hair down to his shoulders" is clearly ridiculous, while the claims that he poisoned his wife and personally murdered the deposed Henry VI are probably also spurious. However, interestingly, when his body was identified early in 2013, it was discovered that he suffered from severe scoliosis of the spine, something which would indeed have given his body a twisted appearance and is the source of the hunchback claims.

Richard III was a ruthless man. He disposed of a number of rivals on his way to the throne, such as ordering the summary executions of Queen Elizabeth Woodville's brother, Earl Rivers and son by her first marriage, Sir Richard Grey, as well as that of Lord Hastings, who had been a friend of Edward IV's. His deposition of his nephew based on the highly dubious claim that he was illegitimate was unprecedented. He did have a better hereditary claim to the throne than Henry Tudor, but his niece, Elizabeth of York, had an even stronger one.

WINNING THE CROWN

Henry Tudor was still living as an exile in Brittany when word arrived of Edward IV's death in April 1483. The ill-feeling towards Richard over the manner in which he had come to the throne, as well as the disappearance of his two nephews, led many Yorkist supporters to turn towards Henry Tudor.

Edward IV's widow, Elizabeth Woodville, had fled to the sanctuary at Westminster with her daughters. Conveniently, she shared a physician with Margaret Beaufort, with the pair passing secret messages through him. In the summer of 1483, Margaret secured the Yorkist queen's agreement to support Henry in return for his marriage to her eldest daughter. The result was a rebellion against Richard in October 1483, which was swiftly crushed by the king and saw Henry unable even to land his Breton troops when he crossed the Channel. Undeterred, on Christmas Day 1483, he made a solemn vow to marry Princess Elizabeth of York.

From Brittany, Henry Tudor began to send letters to leading figures in the kingdom, signing himself as "H.R." to demonstrate that, as far as he was concerned, he was already King of England. More practically, he asked them "to advance me to the furtherance of my rightful claim, due and lineal inheritance of that crown, and for the just depriving of that homicide and unnatural tyrant, which now unjustly bears dominion over you".

Concerned at his rival's actions, Richard III redoubled his efforts to persuade the Duke of Brittany to hand Tudor over, finally securing an agreement to do this towards the end of 1484. Luckily for Henry, his mother, who had links to the English court, sent a warning. In disguise, he crossed the border into France an hour ahead of pursuing soldiers. Luck was finally on Henry Tudor's side and he was made welcome there, setting up a new court in Paris, surrounded by English exiles.

While in France, Henry began to raise funds, with the King of France providing him with money for up to 4000 men at arms. His mother also set about gathering money and support in England. In August 1485, he sailed from Harfleur, landing at Milford Haven.

Henry immediately sent a message to his stepfather, Lord Stanley (1435–1504), who was a powerful magnate, but had hitherto refused to commit himself to his stepson's cause. Richard III, not unnaturally, suspected Stanley of sympathizing with the invader and had already taken his eldest son, Lord Strange (1460–1503), hostage as a surety of his father's loyalty. Lord Strange's position meant that Stanley was not prepared to fully commit himself to Henry, but he and his brother, Sir William Stanley, both met with the younger man on 21 August, with Lord Stanley agreeing not to support the king. At the same time, he also sent four knights and their men to reinforce Henry's vanguard – a sure sign of his support.

Richard III had been at Nottingham when he heard of Henry's landing and immediately moved to cut off his rival's route to the capital. From Leicester, he marched to a field not far from Market Bosworth. He had a larger army than his rival, but his camp was disorganized. When he woke from a night troubled by bad dreams on the morning of 22 August 1485, Richard found that no breakfast had been prepared for him and that there was no priest available for him to hear mass.

Henry's army was smaller, but he was confident and showed no fear as he rode up and down his line, encouraging his troops and urging them forwards. The Battle of Bosworth Field is poorly documented, but it seems that it was Henry who moved first, after Richard's archers began to fire. While the Earl of Oxford, attacked the wing of the king's army, Henry headed towards the centre of Richard's force.

Richard showed great personal courage and, even when the battle began to turn against him, he refused the offer of a horse to allow him to flee. Instead, he waded deeper into the battle, moving towards Henry and killing his standard bearer, Sir William Brandon. Unfortunately for the last Yorkist king, it was at this moment that Sir William Stanley chose to intervene, with his men helping to drive the king backwards. Overwhelmed, Richard fell in battle, becoming the last king of England to die in combat.

According to tradition, Richard's crown was found lying under a hawthorn bush. It was brought to Lord Stanley, who placed it on his stepson's head, declaring Henry Tudor to have become King Henry VII. The Tudor Dynasty had begun.

2

THE FIRST TUDOR KING

Born 28 January 1457
Died 21 April 1509
Reigned 22 August 1485–21 April 1509

Henry VII had three potential claims to the throne: by descent as the heir to the House of Lancaster, by conquest in battle and through his marriage to Elizabeth of York. Given his wife's superior hereditary claim many people favoured the third claim although Henry himself resisted it, having no wish to be a "king at courtesy", as Francis Bacon termed it in his *History of the Reign of King Henry VII*. Henry VII set about establishing himself as the undisputed King of England and building a stable Tudor dynasty.

HENRY VII

The first Tudor king was still only 28 when he came to the throne, having spent most of his adolescence and early adulthood in Brittany, living precariously as a political exile. He had the most unsettled upbringing of any king of England, something that helped shape his character. According to the author Philippe de Comines (1447–c.1511), the king himself once declared that "from the time he was five years old he had been always a fugitive or a prisoner". It was a life lived "continually between hope and fear", as Edward Hall described it in *Hall's Chronicle*, something which spurred Henry on to action when his moment came. Although treated well in Brittany, he was never able to forget his lack of freedom or status, growing into a suspicious but highly intelligent young man.

He was tall, thin and dark. Surviving portraits tend to show the king in his later years: narrow-faced and thin-lipped. In 1498, when he was in his early 40s, the Spanish ambassador Don Pedro de Ayala wrote a letter to Ferdinand and Isabella of Spain in which he said that the king looked "old for his years, but young for the sorrowful life he has led". Nothing came easily for the young Henry Tudor and retaining the throne and building a stable dynasty were the desires that drove him, above all else, throughout his reign.

Although popular perceptions of Henry are that he was an austere, miser-like figure, he knew how to display himself as a king when circumstances required it. At his coronation, shortly after he came to the throne, he purchased powdered ermine and black furs to augment a black velvet jacket. At the same time, he ordered a surcoat of fine blue cloth and cloth of gold to be made into a long gown. He also wore robes of crimson velvet and crimson satin, with fine Holland cloth used to line his doublets. He appeared every inch a monarch as he made his way into Westminster Abbey, which was decorated with red Lancastrian roses, as well as red dragons to emphasise his claims of descent from the mythical kings of Britain. He was remembered in *Hall's Chronicle* after his death as being "of countenance merry and smiling", as well as being "sober, moderate, honest, affable, courteous, bounteous".

Henry's privy purse expenses show a man who was far from joyless or only devoted to business. He often lost money at cards or playing dice – indicating that he was an enthusiastic but unsuccessful gambler. He employed fools to amuse him as well as minstrels. He also enjoyed watching morris dancers or troupes of players, while masques were regularly staged at his court. In March 1504 he spent the astronomical sum of £30,000 on "diverse precious stones and other jewels that come from beyond the sea" as was reported in Henry VII's Privy Purse Exepenses. He loved the trappings of kingship and was determined to maintain them.

The king was determined to crush the power of the nobility in England. He also ensured that the crown was once again solvent, through a system of devastating taxation and fines. This enriched him, but meant that he was unpopular since, as his subjects became poorer, he became richer. It has been estimated that his income from royal lands and wardships rose by 45 per cent during his reign, while he also supplemented this income with approximately £20,000 per year from taxation. Unlike many of his predecessors, Henry VII died solvent, but it was telling that his son's most popular early act was to execute Richard Empson and Edmund Dudley. These men, who were Henry VII's chief revenue collectors, were despised by the nobility who had been their chief targets.

THE CORONATION OF ELIZABETH OF YORK

Elizabeth of York (1466–1503) as the eldest daughter of Edward IV was widely regarded as the Yorkist heiress. She was at Sheriff Hutton Castle in Yorkshire when Henry VII became king. As he moved southwards to claim his throne, Henry sent Sir Robert Willoughby to gain custody of both Elizabeth and her cousin,

Edward, Earl of Warwick (1475–1499), who was the last male Plantagenet heir. The pair were brought to London, with Warwick sent as a prisoner to the Tower and the princess to the house of Margaret Beaufort, the king's mother.

Henry had always promised to marry Elizabeth when he became king in order to unite the two warring houses of Lancaster and York. However, owing to the fact that the couple were related several times over, it was necessary to wait for a papal dispensation, which arrived in early 1486. At the same time, Henry was loath to appear as though he held the crown solely as the husband of Elizabeth of York: another factor in the delay. They finally married on 18 January 1486, with the new queen falling pregnant either shortly before her marriage or immediately afterwards.

Although he fulfilled his vows to marry the Yorkist princess, Henry was wary of his wife's superior claim to the throne and delayed her coronation for some time. It was unusual for a queen to bear an heir before her coronation – an omission which caused some mutterings of discontent among the supporters of the house of York. Finally, on 22 November 1487, Elizabeth, accompanied by her ladies and much of the nobility of England, sailed from Greenwich to the Tower. The flotilla had a carnival atmosphere, with boats belonging to the mayor, merchants and other dignitaries of London moving down the Thames in procession and decked out with banners and streamers. It was a sight to behold, with the crowds assembled on the banks particularly struck by one barge disguised to appear as a "great red dragon spouting flames of fire into the Thames", according to an anonymous report of the time. Musicians stationed on the boats played as the queen arrived at Tower Wharf, where she was met by her husband.

Two days later, Elizabeth stepped out into the streets of London attended by her sister, Cecily, and mother-in-law, Margaret Beaufort, as well as much of the nobility. The queen, who was a great beauty, was dressed in her finery, wearing a gown of white cloth of gold and damask and a furred mantle, which was fastened with gold and silk lace. Her long golden hair hung loose over her shoulders, something that was permitted only for unmarried maidens and queens – while she wore a circlet of gold studded with precious stones. Riding in a fine litter, she travelled through the city of London towards Westminster, along streets which had been cleaned and covered with tapestries and other hangings for the occasion.

Elizabeth was well received during her procession in London and, the following day, she made her way into Westminster Abbey where she was crowned as queen consort of England. If circumstances had been different, Elizabeth of York might very well have been crowned as England's first ruling queen. As the eldest daughter of Edward IV, she certainly had a better claim to the throne than her husband, but no one in late-15th-century England was prepared to support the claim of a woman. Instead, placid and kindly Elizabeth appears to have been content to be queen only by virtue of her marriage.

Elizabeth also enjoyed centre-stage at the banquet that followed her coronation; the king and his mother dined in private and allowed the queen to dominate. Elizabeth and her guests shared 23 dishes in the first course alone, which included such delicacies as pheasant, swan, capons, lampreys, crane, pike, carp, perch, custard and tarts. An even more lavish second course followed, with rabbit, pheasant, peacock, cocks, partridge, sturgeon, quails, larks, baked quince, as well as jellies in the shape of castles to add spectacle to the table.

EARLY TUDOR DRESS

Tudor England was highly stratified, with costume playing an important part in demonstrating a person's status. It was therefore deemed important that Henry VII dressed to look like a king, displaying himself in fine fabrics and bejewelled. As a result, the Tudor monarchs passed a number of Sumptuary Laws, which set out what a person could and could not wear, with a concern that people would otherwise wear "excessive apparel" in an attempt to appear in the guise of their social betters.

One early sumptuary law declared that "no manner of person of whatever estate, degree, or condition he may be, shall wear any cloth of gold, or silk of purple colour, except the king, the queen, the king's mother, the king's children, his brothers and sisters". Gold and purple denoted royalty to the Tudors. No one below the rank of a duke could wear cloth of gold tissue, while only lords and above could wear "plain cloth of gold". Only knights and their social betters could wear velvet in their doublets and gowns. As a further mark of social status, servants and labourers were not permitted to wear cloth which exceeded the price of two shillings per yard, nor were they to "suffer their wives to wear any clothing that is of higher price than is allowed to their husbands".

Clothes mattered in the highly stratified world of Tudor England, which was also a time of great social mobility.

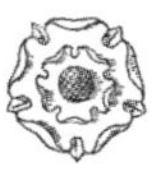

TUDOR LONDON

As king, Henry VII spent much of his time in his capital city, which occupied what Italian visitor Andreas Franciscius described in 1497 as a "convenient and attractive" position. He found much to praise in the city, but also much that was a concern. The streets were badly paved, ensuring that it was impossible for water to drain away, such flooding being something that Franciscius noted"happens very frequently owing to the large number of cattle carrying water, as well as on account of the rain, of which there is a great deal in this island".

Franciscius wrote that the narrow lanes were also filled with "evil-smelling mud", which cannot have made walking around a very pleasant experience. Certainly, it was not something that people wanted walked into their houses or businesses on the feet of visitors, with people in London "accustomed to spread fresh rushes on the floors of all houses, on which they clean the soles of their shoes when they come in".

In around 1488, it was also thought necessary for the mayor to make a proclamation forbidding the dumping of rubbish in the Thames – suggesting that this was common. As well as attempting to keep London clean, the officers of the city were concerned with public morality. The *City of London Letters Books* reported that in 1490, for example, one Christine Houghton, alias Stone, "having been convicted as a common bawd and common strumpet" was ordered to leave the city. When she was discovered to have returned, she was sentenced to two hours in the pillory – a type of stocks designed to humiliate the victim – before being sent to prison for a year and a day.

In spite of the presence of high numbers of foreign visitors and tradesmen, Tudor Londoners had a good deal of suspicion for foreigners, showing what Franciscius termed "fierce tempers" on occasion, particularly towards Italian visitors or Flemish merchants. Nonetheless, international trade was essential to the city, although foreigners could find themselves discriminated against in an attempt to protect English interests. During Henry VII's reign, the mayor of London determined that no foreign baker should be allowed to sell bread within the city after noon "under pain of forfeiting the said bread", according to the *City of London Letters Books*. Similarly, when the English skinners, who prepared animal skins and hides, of London began to struggle to find work, it was ruled "that no stranger nor foreigner hereafter take upon him the occupation of the said Craft of Skinners". Those who were not of English descent often sought to assimilate. The printer, Richard Faques, who originally hailed from France, gradually anglicised the spelling of his surname until he arrived at Fawkes.

London was a crowded, dirty city, but also one at the centre of trade and social life in England. The trades were represented by guilds, which were associations that both regulated the crafts and protected the rights of their members. London had been home to many guilds in the medieval period, and more continued to be founded in Tudor times. In 1486, for example, a licence was given for the foundation of a new guild of bakers, which was to be run by an elected master and four wardens. As well as providing support for bakers who had fallen on hard times, the guild was also intended to aid members.

RICHMOND PALACE

Henry VII was prepared to spend money on luxuries in order to display himself as a monarch. There had been a palace at Sheen, close to the Thames in Surrey, since the medieval period. In December 1497 Henry VII and his family were staying at the palace when it caught fire, burning to the ground. Although it was a traumatic event for the king and queen, who had to leave the burning palace in the night, it gave Henry the opportunity to build a new, modern palace on the site.

Richmond, which was named after Henry's Yorkshire earldom, became his favourite palace. During its rebuilding, between 1497 and 1507, he spent over £14,000 to ensure that it was magnificent. It was built on the site of its predecessor, between the river and Richmond Green. It was entered through a gateway that still survives, which led into a large courtyard surrounded by buildings. Through another gateway, there was a smaller, more intimate central court in which the chapel stood on the left and the great hall on the right. A fountain was placed in the centre.

The great hall was magnificent at over 12 meters (40 feet) high and 30 metres (100 feet) long. Inside, the statues of famous English kings looked down on visitors – with Henry VII prominently situated among his illustrious predecessors. In all its grandeur it was also a comfortable residence, with the king and queen's apartments close together in a building that overlooked the gardens. The king could spend time in his park or gardens, playing chess, bowls or tennis. It was the height of comfort and modernity, and it was here, in the palace in which he spent most of his time, that the king eventually died.

TUDOR HOUSES

Richmond Palace was built as a monument to the glory of the Tudor dynasty, but most people in England lived in considerably more humble dwellings.

Although they sound grand, manor houses, which were occupied by the gentry, tended to be small. The manor of Asfordby in Lincolnshire, for example, contained only eight rooms in which the lord, his wife, children and servants lived. There was a hall, which was the hub of household life and was where many members of the household slept on rolled mats. In the 16th century, the hall at Asfordby contained only a folding table, a long carved settle for sitting on and a chair for the head of the house, as well as a painted canvas hanging to decorate the dais on which he sat. There were a number of sitting rooms. These doubled as bedrooms, with the bed curtains drawn closed when the family rose in the morning. The household at Asfordby contained no books, but there was a very grand collection of plates for display. For their devotions, the family had an alabaster head of St John the Baptist – the only ornament in the household.

Even prominent courtiers lived in houses that would be considered spartan today. An inventory of the household goods of well-known adventurer Sir Peter Carew, for example, comfortably fits on one side of parchment, with items such as "three old bedsteads", chamber pots and plates listed.

Lower down the social scale, houses were even more cramped. In cities, owners sought to increase their space by building first floors butting out over the street. When houses that faced each other had such jetties, it made the street below appear dark and tunnel-like. In the countryside, peasant houses were built of wattle and daub with thatched roofs. Some had two storeys, although most did not. There were also usually open hearths rather than fireplaces, causing many houses to be smoke filled. There would be little furniture or possessions in such houses and they hardly differed from medieval dwellings.

LAMBERT SIMNEL AND PERKIN WARBECK

Henry VII's victory at Bosworth Field is now heralded as the end of the Wars of the Roses, but this was not how it appeared to all his contemporaries. The early years of the first Tudor's reign were plagued by claimants from the house of York, whether genuine or pretenders. Two of the most dangerous were Lambert Simnel (c.1477–1534) and Perkin Warbeck (1474–1499).

Simnel was but a young boy when he emerged in 1487. He claimed to be Edward IV's nephew, Edward Plantagenet, Earl of Warwick, who was at that time a prisoner in the Tower of London. Simnel had been well-schooled in how to behave and even a public event, in which the real Warwick was led out from the Tower, failed to diminish support for him. Simnel was aided both by Edward IV's sister, Margaret of York, Duchess of Burgundy (1446–1503) and her nephew, John de la Pole, Earl of Lincoln (1462–1487). They probably intended to use the boy as a pawn to depose Henry before Lincoln, who had been named as heir to the throne by Richard III, took his place.

Simnel and Lincoln arrived in England in May 1487 and began raising men. They met the king in battle at Stoke on 16 June 1487. For Henry it was a decisive victory, with Lincoln – the last credible Yorkist claimant – dying in the field. The young Lambert Simnel survived, but Henry was prepared to show mercy. He knew that the boy was a mere puppet, as well as understanding the propaganda value of disproving his claims to royal blood. Instead of the Tower, Simnel was put to work in the royal kitchens as a menial servant. In this, however, he was considerably luckier than the next pretender to claim Henry's crown.

Margaret of York was determined to topple Henry Tudor. When news of the defeat at Stoke reached her in Burgundy Hall reported that she, "like a dog reverting to her old vomit, began to devise and spin a new web, like a spider that daily weaveth when his caul is torn". Perkin Warbeck, a handsome and intelligent young man of low birth, first appeared at her court in 1490. Coached by his "aunt", he caused a considerable stir with the claim that he was, in fact, Richard, Duke of York, the younger of the two princes in the Tower, who was presumed to have died in 1483. According to Warbeck he had, "escaped by God's great might out of the Tower of London", before being "secretly conveyed over the sea to divers other countries, there remaining certain years as unknown".

Warbeck was handsome and charming and it suited some to recognize his claims. Margaret of Burgundy was enthusiastic in welcoming her "nephew", offering him aid and ensuring that he was similarly recognized by her stepdaughter's husband, the powerful Archduke Maximilian (1459–1519).

Henry VII was quickly able to ascertain Warbeck's lowly real identity, but the young man posed a considerable threat. With Margaret's coaching, he proved convincing and, in 1495, he visited Scotland where he was duly recognized by James IV (1473–1513) and permitted to marry his kinswoman, Lady Catherine Gordon (1474–1537). He could also count on some support in England: the hitherto loyal Sir William Stanley (1435–1495), brother of the king's own stepfather, was executed for treason when it was discovered that he had been in contact with the pretender.

In the end, Warbeck's claims came to nothing and he was captured in 1497 when he attempted to invade England. Unlike the hapless Lambert Simnel, there was to be no mercy for Perkin Warbeck and he was executed, alongside the innocent Edward Plantagenet, Earl of Warwick, in 1499.

PRINTING COMES TO TUDOR ENGLAND

William Caxton, born c.1415 and died in 1492, was responsible for bringing the printing press to England. This large wooden contraption was the greatest invention of the age. A sheet of paper would be inserted into a holder over a board containing metal letters covered in ink. With the turn of a handle, the printer would force the paper onto the letters, printing a page, then this was removed and a new sheet inserted. Although it was a laborious process, printing was still considerably faster than copying by hand. It also ensured that copies had fewer errors and allowed for the mass production of books for the first time in history.

Caxton set up his own printing works in London. He began to print books in 1473, although it was in the Tudor era that the quantity and variety of printed books exploded. By the 1490s books could be produced cheaply and sold to a wide audience, with booksellers stocking diverse works from religious treatises to Geoffrey Chaucer's *The Canterbury Tales*.

PRINCE ARTHUR

Elizabeth of York was either pregnant at the time of her marriage to Henry VII in January 1486 or she conceived immediately afterwards. The king was anxious to stress the Tudor family's links to the ancient mythical kings of Britain and, as such, insisted that his eldest child be born at Winchester, which was the ancient Anglo-Saxon capital and a city with strong associations with King Arthur. On 20 September 1486 Elizabeth gave birth to a son, who was named Arthur. The boy, who was the eldest of eight children, was raised in his own household as Prince of Wales.

Arthur was betrothed as an infant to Catherine of Aragon (1485–1536), the youngest daughter of Ferdinand and Isabella of Spain. She was raised in her parents' kingdom to be a queen of England, while the boy, Arthur, was encouraged to correspond with her lovingly, writing to the "most illustrious and most excellent lady, my dearest spouse" and speaking of the "earnest desire I feel to see your Highness". In return, Catherine sent him "sweet letters" in her own hand, while Arthur declared – to a girl he had never met – the "ardent love" he felt for her.

THE LOSS OF AN HEIR

The 15-year-old Prince Arthur married Catherine of Aragon in London on 14 November 1501, before the young couple set out for Ludlow, where they were to live. Arthur had always been the focus of Henry's hopes for his dynasty and he was stunned the following April to hear of the sudden death of his eldest son from sweating sickness.

Henry was informed privately of his son's death and immediately sent for his wife, declaring "that he and his Queen would take the painful sorrows together". Elizabeth's first thought was to comfort her husband, reminding him that "my lady his mother had never no more children but him only, and that God by his grace had ever preserved him, and brought him where that he was". She reminded Henry that they still had a surviving son and two living daughters and that they were "both young enough" to produce more children.

Henry took comfort in this and, after a while, the queen returned to her own chamber, where "natural and motherly remembrance of that great loss smote her so sorrowful to the heart" that her attendants sent for the king to comfort her. He came at once, reminding her of all she had said to him and that "he for his part would thank God for his son, and would she would do in like wise".

It had been some years since Elizabeth, who was often ill in pregnancy, had borne a child. With Arthur's death, she sought to conceive again, falling pregnant almost immediately. On 2 February 1503 she bore a short-lived daughter, Catherine, before dying herself on 11 February – her 37th birthday.

Although Henry considered making a second marriage later in his reign, he never took a new bride. His son, Prince Henry, was created Prince of Wales following Arthur's death, while his eldest daughter, Margaret (1489–1541), married James IV, the King of Scots, with her descendants following the Tudors to the English throne in 1603. The possibility of Margaret's accession had, in fact, been raised with Henry before her marriage. He declared that England should not fear being ruled from Edinburgh, since "Scotland would be but an accession to England, and not England to Scotland, for that the greater would draw the less". This later proved to be the case.

SWEATING SICKNESS – A TUDOR PLAGUE

Prince Arthur was carried off by sweating sickness, a mysterious and highly dangerous disease that arrived in England at around the time that Bosworth Field was fought. It was probably a type of influenza.

Outbreaks of sweating sickness came suddenly and with alarming speed. According to *Hall's Chronicles*, "this malady was so cruel that it killed some within three hours, some within two hours, some merry at dinner and dead at supper". The second Tudor monarch, Henry VIII, had a particular fear of the illness. An outbreak in 1517 – which raged from July to December – caused him to break off his summer progress as it began to kill members of his court. Henry, who was always anxious about his health, kept himself apart from the others "with a small company". He cancelled his grand Christmas court for fear that visitors would bring the infection with them.

Since it was "so fervent and infectious", it was a major threat, with some towns losing up to half their population in the second half of 1517 alone. The disease vanished as suddenly as it had arrived after an outbreak in 1551.

The loss of Prince Arthur to sweating sickness in 1502 changed the course of English history. Determined that his surviving son should succeed him, Henry VII kept him close to him at court. The boy was approaching his 18th birthday when the king died on 21 April 1509.

3

HENRY VIII, ADONIS OF FRESH COLOUR

Born 28 June 1491
Died 28 January 1547
Reigned 21 April 1509–28 January 1547

Henry VII had never been a charismatic king and his death went largely unlamented in England. Instead, people looked towards his 17-year-old son, who resembled his Yorkist mother and grandfather in appearance. Even as a teenager, Henry VIII, who came to the throne in April 1509, was a fine specimen, with contemporaries such as the poet John Skelton (1460–1529) raving abou him as "a fresh Adonis", and Lord Mountjoy (1478–1534) describing him as a "new and auspicious star" in a letter to Desiderius Erasmus (1466–1536) in 1509.

HENRY VIII'S APPEARANCE

Henry VIII is a familiar figure from paintings, standing regal and larger than life as he stares out from the canvas. In childhood already he showed considerable promise. The Dutch scholar, Erasmus, who visited him in 1499, declared that the eight-year-old had "already something of royalty in his demeanour". Henry was highly intelligent, sending a note to his illustrious visitor while he sat at dinner to request that the scholar write something for him.

By 1504, when Henry was just entering his teenage years, the Spanish ambassador recorded that the prince was often in his father's company and was a child who "deserves all love". After Arthur's death, Henry VII had been loath to let his surviving son out of his sight, ensuring that the boy learned statecraft from his father – the best tutor he could possibly have. As far as the Spanish ambassador was concerned "if he [Henry VII] lives ten years longer he will leave the Prince furnished with good habits, and with immense riches and in as happy circumstances as man can be".

When he came to the throne Henry was clean-shaven, fair-haired, tall and athletic. According to one contemporary, the young king was "the handsomest potentate I ever set eyes on". He was "above the usual height, with an extremely fine calf to his leg, his complexion very fair and bright, with auburn hair combed straight and short, in the French fashion, and a round face so very beautiful, that it would become a pretty woman". Henry also dressed to impress in costly fabrics, such as silk or velvet.

In his youth, Henry was an athlete, taking part enthusiastically in jousts and court entertainments. A leg injury sustained in 1536, when he was in his mid-40s, put paid to this and led to him becoming the overweight and ungainly character of popular legend. In 1509, however, he appeared the perfect model of a Renaissance prince, as Henry himself was well aware. On one occasion, he pulled the Venetian ambassador aside, asking him to "Talk with me awhile!" He then questioned the emissary asking,

"The King of France, is he as tall as I am?" and "Is he as stout?", with the ambassador assuring the young king that he cut the finer figure. Pleased, Henry then asked "What sort of leg has he?", before opening his own doublet to display his thigh declaring, "Look here! And I have also a good calf to my leg".

Rivalry with Francis I of France (1494–1547), who was of a similar age, dominated Henry's thoughts as he sought to present himself in the best manner that he could. A little later, on hearing that Francis had a beard, Henry allowed his to grow red and thick, with an onlooker commenting that "he has now got a beard which looks like gold".

THE KING'S WARDROBE

Henry VIII liked to dress to impress. Wardrobe accounts survive from the early years of his reign, giving a flavour of what the king chose to wear. He particularly enjoyed exotic clothes, holding items in French, Italian, Spanish and Turkish styles. He owned many items of footwear, purchasing at least one pair of comfortable velvet shoes a week. Around court, the king would sometimes wear slippers. He was sensitive about his clothes. Later, one of the charges laid against his second wife, Anne Boleyn, was that she had laughed at the king's attire.

MAGNIFICENT JEWELS

An inventory of his possessions, taken after his death, shows the splendour in which Henry VIII lived. He loved jewels; a golden crown decorated with sapphires, rubies and diamonds was just one of his treasures. He had golden collars, as well as bracelets and other works of finery. He also kept some items to remind him of his youth. At his death, the king still kept costumes from the masques that he had participated in as a young man, including

Turkish coats made of cloth of gold and sleeves of blue satin. He also kept masks from the performances – both with and without beards.

A KEEN SPORTSMAN

As his father's precious only surviving son, Henry VIII had been strictly protected before he came to the throne. The young prince was fascinated with jousting and other feats of martial prowess, but was not allowed to take part. Instead, he haunted the tournament grounds, seeking out the competitors "to speak of arms and of other defence", as described in the contemporary poem, "The Justes of the Moneths of May and June". He longed for the day when he could participate himself.

On 12 January 1510 the new king finally got the opportunity and, with his friend, Sir William Compton (1482–1528), he took part in a tournament in disguise. Henry's debut was spectacular and he broke many staves in the jousts, winning the praise of the crowd. Unfortunately, it was never possible for the king to be entirely inconspicuous. Someone in the crowd knew that he was participating and, when Compton fell down injured, they cried out "God save the King", forcing Henry to reveal himself and reassure those around him that he was unhurt.

With his first attempt at a tournament a success, Henry began to appear regularly. Although there was a natural tendency for those around him to quietly let him win, he was a proficient jouster, performing reasonably well in 1520 against French opponents determined to humble him. Within a year of his accession there were reports that Henry spent two days a week at such sports. He also enjoyed hunting and other pursuits, spending much of his time active during the early years of his reign.

HENRY VIII AND CATHERINE OF ARAGON

On 3 June 1509 the 17-year-old Henry VIII privately married his sister-in-law, Catherine of Aragon (1485–1536). No one was more shocked at the sudden turn of events than the bride herself, who had almost allowed herself to give up hope of ever becoming Queen of England.

Catherine of Aragon, who was more than five years older than her husband, was the youngest daughter of Ferdinand (1452–1516), King of Aragon and his wife, Isabella (1451–1504), the reigning queen of Castile. The couple were famous as the Catholic Kings of Spain, who funded Christopher Columbus and drove the Moors out of Granada. They agreed to marry their daughter to Prince Arthur when the two children were infants, raising Catherine in the certain knowledge that her future lay in England. Even after Arthur's sudden death in April 1502, she remained as a widow in England, promised to his younger brother.

The death of her mother in October 1504 diminished Catherine's status. On 27 July 1505, Henry VII made his son secretly renounce his betrothal before the Bishop of Winchester, and began covertly looking for a more prestigious match. All the time Catherine waited, often so short of funds that she had to beg her father for money to buy food. She found herself in such straitened circumstances that "about my person, I have nothing for chemises; wherefore, by your highness' leave, I have now sold some bracelets to get a dress of black velvet, for I was all but naked".

All this changed with the sudden death of Henry VII. His son was anxious to assert his status as an adult sovereign and the best way to do this was as a married man. Catherine was a conveniently available princess, as well as a woman that Henry VIII knew well and found attractive. She was fair-haired, small and pretty, and the king believed himself in love. Catherine also fell in love with him, and the couple shared a coronation shortly after their marriage. For Catherine of Aragon it was a fairy-tale ending to her years of waiting. To add to her joy, she fell pregnant rapidly.

ROBIN HOOD AND HIS MERRY MEN

Henry and Catherine presided over a lively court, with the king delighting in surprising his queen. One morning in 1510, while the court was staying at Westminster, Robin Hood and 11 of his merry men burst into the queen's chamber. Catherine and her ladies were, said Hall, "abashed, as well for the strange sight, as also for their sudden coming", but they danced with the masked intruders before the outlaws left the way they had come.

Catherine and her ladies always played along, knowing full well that it was Henry and some of his friends. The early court of Henry VIII was filled with music and dancing, with the young couple determined to enjoy themselves.

MUSIC

Henry VIII loved music and was a gifted composer. He owned many musical instruments, some of which he could play himself. As well as clavichords, lutes and virginals, he also owned bagpipes and flutes.

Some of his songs survive. While there is no evidence that he composed the famous "Greensleeves", he did write "Pastance with Good Company" recalling his youthful dalliances:

> Pastance with good company
> I love and shall until I die
> Grudge who will, but none deny
> So god be pleased this life will I

For my pastance,
Hunt, sing, and dance,
My heart is set,
All goodly sport
To my comfort
Who shall me let?

Henry employed his own troops of minstrels to entertain him. Upper-class girls were also taught to sing and encouraged to play instruments in the hope that this would improve their chances of marriage.

CARDINAL THOMAS WOLSEY (1473–1530)

In the early years of his reign, Henry VIII focused more on enjoying himself than attending to business. As a result, he relied on ministers, such as Thomas Wolsey, who had risen in the church from humble origins as the son of a butcher from Ipswich.

Wolsey had begun his meteoric assent when he was appointed as one of Henry VII's chaplains in 1507. Henry VIII had a talent for recognizing ability and promoted the churchman, making him his almoner in November 1509 before appointing him to the royal council in June 1510.

Wolsey was a man of great organizational ability, which he used to excellent effect in 1513 when he helped to arrange the logistics for the king's French military campaign. The following year he was appointed as Bishop of Lincoln and only a few months later became Archbishop of York. In September 1515, the churchman became a cardinal. He was soon also Lord Chancellor, and gained authority over the English church in 1518 when he became papal legate. It was only the longevity of William Warham (1450–1532), Henry VII's Archbishop of Canterbury, that stopped him from achieving the premier English. In any case, with his papal appointments, Wolsey outranked Warham anyway and even had ambitions to become Pope himself, although this came to nothing.

When Henry had been on the throne for a decade, it was widely believed that he was under Wolsey's control; one contemporary, Guistiniani, the Venetian ambassador to England, wrote that "the Cardinal is the person who rules both the King and the entire kingdom". At first, he had always scrupulously said "His Majesty will do so and so" when petitioned on a particular subject, but, as time went by, he began to forget himself, first by saying "We shall do so and so", before, finally, merely replying "I shall do so and so".

It was no wonder that Wolsey was resented by much of the established nobility and others about the court. The poet, John Skelton, who bitterly resented his own lack of royal favour, summed up the mood by referring to the Cardinal as a "mastiff cur" and a "butcher's dog". He also poked fun at the power that Wolsey wielded from his mansion at Hampton Court, declaring:

> Why come ye not to court?
> To which court?
> To the king's court,
> Or to Hampton Court?

As far as Skelton and many of his contemporaries was concerned, "the king's court shall have the excellence, but Hampton Court hath the pre-eminence".

Wolsey was not always negatively portrayed, with references in sources to his benevolence and charity. He was also acquisitive and even the king was jealous of the splendour in which he lived. In fact, Henry forced the cardinal to exchange Hampton Court for the less luxurious Richmond Palace. Wolsey, who was popularly reviled for his "great pride" as noted in the contempoary ballad, "A ballet of ye deth of ye Cardynall", was mourned by few when he fell from power in 1529.

THE FIELD OF THE CLOTH OF GOLD

In June 1520, Henry crossed the English Channel for a summit with his rival, Francis I of France. The English, who numbered 5,172, made their camp at Guisnes, while the French contingent of 6,000 people, male and female, stayed at nearby Ardes. The two kings met on 7 June, dismounting from their horses and embracing. They then retired to a tent made of cloth of gold to speak together pleasantly like old friends.

Both kings sought to show the splendour of their courts and the people who served them, with grand jousts beginning on 11 June. Francis's wife, Claude (1499–1524), along with her ladies, watched from a specially constructed gallery beside the tiltyard, as did Catherine of Aragon and her sister-in-law, Mary Tudor, who was herself a former queen of France. Both kings took part in the week's jousts, showing their prowess as they sought to outdo each other in feats of arms.

For Henry, the celebrations were marred somewhat on 13 June when wrestling was held, since it was deemed too windy to joust. Henry, a larger man than his French counterpart, unsportingly challenged Francis to a match and was embarrassed to be unceremoniously thrown to the ground by the French king. He was perhaps gladder than most when the jousts recommenced the next day.

As well as sport, the Field of the Cloth of Gold – which was named for the splendour of the tents and pavilions erected by the two monarchs – included banquets and entertainments. On 11 June Francis set out to dine at Guisnes with Catherine of Aragon, while Henry rode to Ardes to dine with Queen Claude. Among the French queen's ladies was a young Englishwoman named Anne Boleyn, who had arrived in France some years before. She and the other French ladies danced with Henry while the queen looked on, serene in a dress of gold cloth embroidered with jewels. At the same time, at Guisnes, Francis displayed his charm by greeting each of the ladies with a kiss. He unchivalrously omitted only three or five women "that were old and not fair" according to Hall.

Six days later, the two kings switched places again to dine, with Henry appearing before Claude disguised in an old-fashioned gown of blue satin with a mask and false beard of Dutch gold. There was a carnival atmosphere as Henry rode through the streets of Ardes accompanied his own troupe of minstrels.

The glory of the meeting and the holiday atmosphere it engendered could not last forever. On 23 June a temporary chapel, which sprang up overnight on the site of the tournament site, was used by Cardinal Wolsey to celebrate mass for both the French and English. That evening the kings again dined with their counterpart's queens, with Henry and Francis timing their return to their camps to ensure that they could meet and embrace on the road home.

This was the end of the celebration and the grandest event of Henry's long reign. Even the austere Bishop Fisher, who had been a chaplain to Henry's grandmother, Margaret Beaufort, was awed by the spectacle, commenting that all the gorgeous costumes, pastimes, banquets and feats of arms, among the other splendours of the meeting "assuredly were wonderful sights as for this world".

TUDOR FOOD

Banquets featured heavily at the Field of the Cloth of Gold, but everyday fare in Tudor England could be equally rich and exotic. Noble households purchased great quantities of food. Meat, such as pork, chicken, lamb, venison and rabbit, was eaten in large quantities. On Fridays and in Lent fish was prepared instead, with a wide variety consumed. As well as salmon, crab and cod, river fish such as pike were enjoyed. Eels were also a delicacy. Freshwater fish could be particularly economic, since many manors had fishponds to help feed the household. Bread was often baked at home, with quantities of yeast, eggs and flour brought in for baking.

Poorer households ate seasonal produce, grown in their kitchen gardens. Root crops, such as radishes, beetroots and carrots dominated, along with beans and cabbages. Carrots would have been purple, yellow or white, with orange varieties unknown in the sixteenth century.

THE SPANISH CONQUEST OF MEXICO

While Henry VIII lavished his time and energies on sports and entertainments, the world began to grow larger in his and his subjects' perceptions. The Americas were "discovered" in 1492 by Christopher Columbus, in a Spanish-backed expedition. This gave Spain a considerable advantage in tapping the resources of the New World. In 1519, an army, led by Hernando Cortés (1485–1547), arrived in modern-day Mexico, which was then at the heart of the great Aztec Empire. The Aztec Emperor, Montezuma (c.1460–1520), first thought that the Spanish were gods, something that allowed the conquistadors to enter the heart of his empire. Cortés was able to capture Montezuma, who was killed the following year. It did not take the Spaniards, who were armed with guns and mounted on horses, long to conquer to empire itself. This gave them access to the great treasures of the New World.

4

THE QUEST FOR AN HEIR

When he came to the throne in 1509, Henry VIII was the only living male Tudor. His mother, Elizabeth of York, had been widely regarded as the heir to the throne, but no one ever seriously considered that she could wear the crown herself, since England had never had a ruling queen. Henry VIII was as anxious to secure his dynasty as his father had been, but it took him nearly 30 years to father a healthy male heir.

PRINCE HENRY

Catherine of Aragon conceived soon after her marriage, miscarrying a daughter in January 1510. She became pregnant again quickly, bearing a son on New Year's Day 1511.

The baby, who was named Henry after his father, was the best New Year's present that Catherine could give her husband. When the birth was announced, London erupted in rejoicing, with bonfires lit and wine distributed freely to the citizens, many of whom went in procession to church in celebration. The 19-year-old king was thrilled and, on 12 February 1511 took part in a grand tournament before the court and the queen. Henry, who was on the best terms with his wife that he would ever be, jousted as "Sir Loyal Heart", with his livery decorated with their entwined initials. At the same time, he composed a song, which he set down in his manuscript music book, stating his joy at the birth:

Adieu; adieu le company!
I trust we shall meet oftener,
Vive le Katerine et vive le prince
Le infant Rosary.

The prince was given a grand household to attend him, including a clerk of the signet and a keeper of his wardrobe who were appointed on 21 February 1511. Sadly, these men had little time to enjoy their offices. On 23 February 1511, while at Richmond Palace, the baby died, having lived for less than two months.

Both parents mourned for the child, Edward Hall (1497–1547) in *Hall's Chronicle*, remarked that "the king like a wise prince, took this dolorous chance wondrous wisely". In order to comfort Catherine, who "made much lamentation", he bore the loss stoically and helped to "mitigate" his wife's "sorrow". He ordered a grand funeral for his son at Westminster Abbey. Touchingly, at Easter he also arranged to pay an annuity to one Elizabeth Pointes, "late nurse unto our dearest son the Prince".

Infant mortality was devastatingly high in Tudor England and Henry and Catherine's experience was not unusual. The queen was pregnant again in September 1511, but suffered another miscarriage. On 8 October 1513 she bore a second son, who James Bannisius, Imperial Agent to the Lord Albert of Carpi, said "will inherit the crown, the other son having died". Sadly, this second prince died shortly after birth. A third son was born in late December 1514 or early January 1515, but died quickly. As Henry began to give up hope of having living issue with his queen, she conceived again in the spring of 1515.

 PREGNANCY AND LABOUR

Without modern medicine, it was impossible to confirm pregnancy until the baby was felt to move in the womb, which was known as quickening. Some medical conditions could mimic pregnancy and phantom pregnancies, where a woman believed herself to be pregnant, were not that uncommon. Once a pregnancy was confirmed, a woman would appear in open-laced gowns, or dresses with an added panel of fabric.

Childbirth was a female preserve, attended by the labouring woman's mother, aunts, sisters and other relatives. Midwives also attended at most births. They did not require any formal training, with the only qualification necessary to practice being a licence from a bishop, in order to ensure that they were of fit character in the event that they were called upon to baptise a sickly infant.

It was commonly believed that a birthing room should be kept warm, with a roaring fire in the hearth and curtains or shutters over any windows. After birth, a child would be tightly swaddled in cloth and laid in a crib. Given the high infant death rate, the baby was christened as soon as possible, often on the day of the birth. Higher-status women usually hired wet nurses to suckle their infants, although lower-status women breastfed their own children. It was commonly believed that a wet nurse would pass something of her character and temperament to the child in her milk, ensuring that the appointment of a nurse involved careful consideration.

A ROYAL BIRTH

Most Tudor women would assist at a birth during their lifetime, as well as experience labour themselves at least once. For royal women, a birth was particularly elaborate. Henry VII's mother, Margaret Beaufort, prepared a set of Ordinances for a Royal Birth in 1486 in advance of the arrival of her first grandchild.

No detail was too small for Margaret. She went so far as to set out the furnishings and decorations to be prepared in the queen's chamber, declaring that that room should be hung with tapestries covering the walls, ceiling and windows. If a queen wished to have natural light or fresh air, one window could be uncovered, a small concession that cannot have helped much to ease the stuffiness of the birthing chamber.

Around a month before the expected birth, the queen ceremonially took to her chamber after hearing mass. Once inside, she entered an entirely female world, since, as specified by Margaret Beaufort's Ordinances for a Royal Birth, "none [were] to come unto the great Chamber but Women". During the lying-in, women took over all the male roles in the queen's household, such as that of butler. Men could only come with "needful things" "unto the great chamber door" where "the Women Officers shall receive it there of them".

The queen remained cloistered away until she was churched, a ceremony that involved a priest blessing the new mother, and which was held some weeks after the birth. She could then return to everyday life until her next confinement.

A CAESAREAN SECTION

Not all births went according to plan, with both infant and maternal mortality alarmingly high during the Tudor period. When things went wrong in childbirth, there was little that the midwives or doctors could do.

Some contemporaries believed that Henry VIII's third wife, Jane Seymour, was forced to undergo a Caesarean section when she gave birth in October 1537, with a contemporary ballad recording that her doctors "opened her two sides, and the baby was found". Such rumours were false since Jane, who died of puerperal – or childbed – fever, survived the birth by 12 days. This would have been impossible if the child had been born by Caesarean.

Caesarean sections where the mother died during labour were known in Tudor England and had been performed since antiquity. A child born in such a way was not expected to survive, with the operation carried out to allow baptism. In the late 16th century, physician Françoise Rousset wrote a treatise advocating the operation's use on living women. Given the lack of anaesthetic and poor knowledge of hygiene, it is highly unlikely that any Tudor women could survive such a procedure, although the babies sometimes did. Such children were referred to as "not of woman born" or, more accurately, simply "the fortunate".

PRINCESS MARY AND HENRY FITZROY

On 18 February 1516, Catherine of Aragon gave birth to her only child that would survive to adulthood, Princess Mary. The child's sex was disappointing, with the Venetian ambassador writing after the birth that he would congratulate the king shortly, but that "had it been a son, I should have already done so". After so many disappointments, Henry was philosophical when the ambassador eventually came to him, declaring that "we are both young: if it was a daughter this time, by the grace of God the sons will follow".

Henry was optimistic, but Catherine, at the age of 30, was past the first flush of youth by Tudor standards. It took two years for her to conceive again, bearing a further daughter. This was greeted with what the Venetian Ambassador Sebastian Giustinian described as "the vexation of everybody" on 10 November 1518. This second daughter failed to survive and Catherine did not fall pregnant again.

The loss of Catherine's final baby was thrown into sharp relief by the fact that another woman was in the early stages of pregnancy with the king's child. Bessie Blount (1498–1540), a young Shropshire gentlewoman, had come to court to serve Catherine and soon became Henry's mistress. In June 1519 she bore a son, who was named Henry Fitzroy (1519–1536) and immediately acknowledged by the king, with Cardinal Wolsey standing as his godfather. For Henry VIII, this was the first proof that he could sire a healthy son. He ensured that the boy was royally brought up, with a reorganization of Princess Mary's household, allowing some of her staff to transfer to the service of the new baby.

Henry Fitzroy, as an illegitimate child, had no rights to the crown, but the king doted on him. On the morning of 18 June 1525, the six-year-old boy was brought to Bridewell Palace where he was created Duke of Richmond and Somerset by his devoted father. Shortly afterwards, Fitzroy was sent with a large household to Sheriff Hutton Castle in Yorkshire, to nominally rule over the northern part of the kingdom.

Henry Fitzroy's elevation alarmed the queen, and Henry dismissed three of her Spanish ladies in an attempt to silence her protests, obliging her "to submit and to have patience". Catherine, as the daughter of a powerful female sovereign, was raising her child to be a future queen of England and feared the king's favouritism towards his illegitimate son. Princess Mary was nine years old in 1525 and was a small, pretty and well-proportioned girl. Like Fitzroy, she was intelligent, with the statesman Ralph Sadler (1507–1587) commenting that she was "of her age as goodly a child, as ever I have seen".

Perhaps in an attempt to pacify the queen, later that year Henry sent their daughter westwards to Ludlow with a large household full of people the clergyman Richard Sampson described as "diverse persons of gravity". Although Mary was never formally created Princess of Wales, Ludlow Castle was the traditional seat of the heirs to the throne and the base from which Wales was governed. By dispatching her there, Henry sent out a strong message that, for the time being, his daughter was his most likely successor.

Henry Fitzroy remained a strong contender until his early death on 23 July 1536, only a few weeks before the Earl of Sussex, reflecting on the fact that the king had, by that stage, produced two daughters by two disputed marriages, as well as his illegitimate son, advised "that it would be advisable to prefer the male to the female for the succession to the Crown".

EDUCATION

Early in the 16th century, it became fashionable for upper-class girls to receive an education, something which benefitted Henry VIII's two daughters, Princesses Mary and Elizabeth (Henry VIII's daughter with his second wife, Anne Boleyn), their kinswoman Lady Jane Grey, and other girls of the gentry and nobility.

One of Elizabeth's tutors was Roger Ascham (1515–1568), who published a book called *The Scholemaster* on his revolutionary methods for ensuring that he got the best out of his pupils. Ascham believed that great care should be taken to ensure that the child learned in the correct way, since "these faults, taking once root in youth, be never or hardly, plucked away in age". He was a benign schoolmaster, arguing that a child should be praised when they did well, since "I assure you, there is no whetstone, to sharpen a good wit and encourage a will to learning, as is praise".

He also felt that children who tried their best but made mistakes should not be punished, arguing that scholars should not be made to fear their tutor. As far as Ascham was concerned, it was essential to instill a love of learning into his pupils, something which he achieved with Princess Elizabeth, who continued to read for enjoyment throughout her lifetime. The future Elizabeth I was extremely well educated, speaking French, Spanish and Italian, as well as reading Latin and Greek. She was Ascham's star pupil, with the tutor declaring that she put the young men of England to shame with her "excellent gifts of learning".

Educational provision also improved for children lower down the social scale in Tudor England. A number of grammar schools were founded, with their curriculums based on humanist principles and focusing on Latin and Greek. These tended to cater to sons of the gentry and lower nobility and boys would start at the age of seven. The day at grammar school was a long one – often starting before sunrise and finishing after the sun set. For poorer children, there might be a parish school close to their home, where the vicar would teach them to read or write. Although some tutors, such as Roger Ascham, had enlightened views on punishments most Tudor schoolboys would expect to be beaten if they made an error or misbehaved.

MAGDALEN COLLEGE SCHOOL, OXFORD

During the early Tudor period, Magdalen College School in Oxford offered young boys the best school education that they could get in England. It opened at Easter 1480, moving into its permanent building just inside the gates of Magdalen College, that autumn.

The school offered free tuition to its pupils, who sat at their lessons between 5 am and 5 pm every day, only breaking for breakfast and lunch. The schoolroom, on the ground floor of the two-storey school house, had room for 100 scholars, who were instructed by two tutors. To keep order, the pair used a birch cane to chastise the boys. To be educated there was a great privilege, with the school the first in England to teach classical Latin in accordance with humanist principles, rather than the corrupted Latin of the medieval period. This allowed the scholars to read classical works in the original language. Many of the pupils went on to become bishops and great thinkers, with William Tyndale, who translated the Bible into English, one of the school's alumni.

ANNE BOLEYN (1501–1536)

By the 1520s Henry had lost all hope of fathering a son with Catherine of Aragon. In March 1522, a great masque was held at Greenwich in which seven ladies of the court portrayed the Virtues. The king's lovely younger sister, Mary, took the role of Beauty, while his mistress, Mary Boleyn (1499–1543), played Kindness. Appropriately, as it would transpire, Mary Boleyn's younger sister depicted Perseverance. Mary Boleyn, who was a year or two older than her sister, would serve as the king's mistress for some years. In the 16th century kings were not expected to be faithful to their wives, instead choosing mistresses from among the women at court. In England, a royal mistress had no official role, although they could sometimes influence royal policy through their intimate relationship with the sovereign. Henry VIII was also generous to his mistresses. Mary Boleyn's husband, who was accepting of the relationship, received a number of royal grants and offices, while her father was ennobled as Viscount Rochford in 1525. Once he had tired of a mistress, Henry simply abandoned them in favour of a new lover. Mary Boleyn had supplanted Bessie Blount early in 1522 when Bessie – the mother of the king's illegitimate son – was married off to a wealthy young courtier. Mary Boleyn was similarly discarded not long before Henry began to show an interest in her sister. The Greenwich masque was the 21-year-old

Anne Boleyn's debut at the English court. It was a stunning success, with the gorgeously dressed women defending a mock castle with rose water and comfits as it was stormed by the king and his friends.

Henry VIII paid little attention to the French-educated Anne in 1522, remaining enamoured of her sister. Anne Boleyn was not conventionally beautiful. Claims that she had a sixth finger on one hand are exaggerated, but she did have an extra nail on one finger. She could disguise this easily with the hanging sleeves that were popular at the time. Later, Catherine of Aragon would insist that she join her to play cards, ensuring that her hands were on display. Anne was dark-haired and dark-eyed when the contemporary ideal was that a woman should be fair. Nevertheless, her eyes, which were her best feature, were captivating and, with her French grace, she stood out at court. In 1526, while flirting with the married poet, Sir Thomas Wyatt (1503 –1542), she caught the attention of the king.

Thomas Wyatt referred to Anne as "Fair Brunet" in his works and would later liken his unsuccessful pursuit of her to that of a deer in the chase. One day, while the pair were speaking, he playfully stole a jewel from her, wearing it round his neck as a trophy. At around the same time Henry, who had also become interested in Anne, took a ring from her to wear on his own finger.

The rivalry between the king and his friend came to a head one day when the pair played bowls. During the game, Henry confidently declared that he had won when it was clear that he had not, pointing with the finger on which he wore Anne's ring and declaring "Wyatt, I tell thee it is mine". Wyatt recognized this as a challenge. He reached into his shirt to pull out Anne's jewel, declaring that "If it may like your majesty to give me leave to measure it, I hope it will be mine". Henry, seeing the diamond, angrily broke up the game, declaring "it may be so, but then am I deceived".

At first, Henry only sought to make Anne his mistress, but the object of his affections, who had seen him discard her own sister, refused. Royal mistresses had no status at court. Although their role – as the king's lover – could lead to political influence and financial gain, they were all eventually abandoned. Instead of accepting Henry's offer, she retreated to her home of Hever Castle in Kent, where she was bombarded with ardent love letters. Henry was not used to being refused and it only increased his ardour, and he declared to Anne that:

"For although by absence we are parted it nevertheless keeps its fervency, at least in my case and hoping the like of yours; assuring you that for myself the pangs of absence is already too great, and when I think of the increase of what I must needs suffer it would be well nigh intolerable but for my firm hope in your unchangeable affection".

Henry, who hated writing, sat down to write 17 letters professing his ardent affection. Sometimes he would draw a heart at the end of the letter, enclosing his and Anne's initials within it. The object of his affections, however, continued to refuse him.

Finally, when Henry realized that he could not live without Anne, he offered her the only thing that she would accept: marriage. For Henry, a union with Anne, who was still in her mid-20s, gave the possibility of sons, as well as the ability to finally consummate the relationship. Anne was uneasy, but accepted.

As the king led her out publically as his partner at a court dance on 5 May 1527, neither could have realised that it would be almost six years before they could marry. Henry often danced with his mistresses and this was the first public demonstration of his love for Anne, although few would have realised the significance of the gesture. Later that month, a secret ecclesiastical court opened in London to try the validity of Henry's marriage to Catherine of Aragon.

5

THE KING'S GREAT MATTER

When Henry VIII decided to marry Anne Boleyn in 1527, only one thing stood in his way – his wife. Divorce was not possible in the 16th century, but the king could seek an annulment. He seized upon the Book of Leviticus, which stated that a man who married his brother's widow would be childless. This use of scripture to justify a separation was highly controversial. Notwithstanding the existence of Princess Mary, the Book of Deuteronomy contained an express command for a man to marry his childless brother's widow, making the king's position far from straightforward.

THE BLACKFRIARS TRIAL

Catherine of Aragon had no intention of being discarded and immediately wrote to her nephew, the Holy Roman Emperor, Charles V (1500–1558). Henry's actions threatened Imperial family honour, with Charles declaring that he was prepared to defend his aunt's "just cause". He was well able to do so since, on 16 June 1527 his troops sacked Rome, holding Pope Clement VII (1478–1534) as a virtual prisoner.

The pope had the ultimate authority to rule in the case and Henry sent several embassies, requesting that the case be heard in England. Finally, on 11 June 1528, Clement relented, promising to send Cardinal Campeggio to hear the case. Both Henry VIII and Anne Boleyn were jubilant, not suspecting that Campeggio, who made painfully slow progress towards England, had been instructed to delay matters as much as possible.

The cardinal finally arrived in London on 8 October 1528 and retired immediately to his sick-bed with gout. He spent the Christmas period indisposed before stirring himself to attempt to fulfil his secret orders from the pope: to "persuade the queen to a divorce; and dissuade the king from it, as having either way the end he proposed; yet he failed in both". Both Catherine and Henry were resolute, with Campeggio recalling that the king was so convinced that his marriage was void that "if an angel was to descend from heaven he would not be able to persuade him to the contrary". At the same time, Catherine refused to become a nun, a solution which would have allowed the king to remarry.

With neither party budging, Campeggio was obliged to hear the case himself, convening a legatine court, which was a hearing held under papal authority, with Cardinal Wolsey at Blackfriars on 18 June 1529. To everyone's surprise, the queen heeded their summons, arriving to sit in her chair on the opposite side of the hall to Henry. As the court opened, it became clear that she was anything but compliant. Rising to her feet, Catherine crossed the floor to kneel before her husband. She then made a formal appeal for the case to be heard in Rome, before launching into a long speech, declaring:

"I beseech you for all the love that hath been between us, and for the love of God, let me have justice and right, take of me some pity and compassion, for I am a poor woman and a stranger born out of your dominion. I have here no assured friends, and much less impartial counsel. I flee to you as to the head of justice within this realm."

She continued, asking Henry how she had offended him and declaring that "I take God and all the world to witness that I have been to you a true, humble and obedient wife, ever comfortable to your will and pleasure". She declared that she had always done as he bid her and loved his friends, even when they were her enemies. "This twenty years or more I have been your true wife and by me ye have had diverse children, although it hath pleased God to call them out of this world, which hath been no default of me". The case hinged on whether Catherine had consummated her first marriage to Arthur and she insisted that Henry had found her a virgin, before begging to be allowed to remain as his wife. She then rose and strode out of the hall, declaring that "it is no impartial court for me, therefore I will not tarry".

Catherine's conduct was excruciating for the king, who sat in stony silence. The court continued to convene in the queen's absence but, unbeknownst to Henry, Campeggio had no authority to give a judgment. Finally, to uproar, he stood and revoked the case to Rome. In over two years of waiting, Henry VIII was no further advanced in his attempts to secure his "Great Matter" and marry Anne Boleyn.

CATHERINE OF ARAGON'S VIRGINITY

The key to Henry VIII's case was that Catherine of Aragon, as his sister-in-law, could never validly be his wife. It was therefore crucial to prove that his wife's previous marriage had been consummated.

Catherine always insisted that she had been a virgin when she married Henry in 1509. There were, however, plenty of people prepared to give evidence to the contrary. George, Earl of Shrewsbury, who had been present when Arthur had been conducted to Catherine's chamber on their wedding night, testified that he had always supposed that the marriage had been consummated – he could see no reason why it had not been.

Sir Anthony Willoughby went further, stating that, on the morning after the wedding, Arthur had called to him, saying "Willoughby, bring me a cup of ale, for I have been this night in the midst of Spain". Arthur was heard to boast that "it is good pastime to have a wife".

On the other hand, Catherine was a deeply pious woman and it would seem unlikely that she was lying. Spanish sources also suggest that Arthur had been a poor physical specimen and unlikely to have been able to consummate his marriage.

In any event, the papal dispensation obtained by her parents for her wedding to Henry had stated that her first marriage was "perhaps consummated" which, when combined with a papal brief that Catherine was able to supply from Spain, overcame many of the difficulties regarding her previous marriage to Henry's brother.

THE FALL OF CARDINAL WOLSEY

As the Blackfriars trial broke up, Henry's brother-in-law, the Duke of Suffolk, declared angrily that "Cardinals never did good in England". At that moment, this was a sentiment with which the king heartily agreed and he was as furious with Wolsey as he was with Campeggio at their failure to annul his marriage.

It was in fact Wolsey who provided the only common ground that Catherine of Aragon and Anne Boleyn had, since both women loathed him. Catherine believed that it was the cardinal who had planted the idea of divorce in the king's head. She embarrassed him when he came to speak to her privately by insisting that he give any message to her verbally – in English – in front of her household.

Anne Boleyn had borne a grudge against the cardinal for years after he had broken off her early betrothal to the heir to the Earl of Northumberland. Anne, whom Wolsey referred to as "a serpentine enemy" and "the Night Crow" had the ear of the king and was able to isolate the cardinal from his master. On one occasion, Wolsey arrived at court for a scheduled meeting only to find that Anne had arranged a hunting trip and picnic which necessitated Henry's absence all that day.

Henry was furious with what he perceived to be Wolsey's lack of effort on his behalf. On 9 October 1529, the cardinal was charged with taking orders from a foreign power (the pope) and forced to surrender the great seal and his position as chancellor. He was ordered to retire to Esher and surrendered his goods to the king, throwing himself on his mercy. Henry still had some affection for his old servant, sending his own physician to attend him at Christmas 1529 when he fell ill. He also insisted that the reluctant Anne Boleyn send him a token of comfort.

While Henry had not completely abandoned the cardinal, he refused to see him. At Easter 1530 he ordered him to travel to his diocese of York. Wolsey set out slowly, aware that his enemies continued to dominate the king. He was at Cawood in November 1530 when the young Earl of Northumberland, who was Anne Boleyn's former suitor, arrested him for treason.

Wolsey was brought slowly towards London with his legs tied to his horse. The once proud Cardinal had become an object of pity, complaining that "had I served God as diligently as I had done the King, he would not have given me over, in my grey hairs". He never made it to London, dying at Leicester on 29 November 1530. He was rumoured to have taken poison to avoid the executioner's block, and while he may have died of natural causes, he died an old and broken man.

THREE'S A CROWD

Henry and Catherine continued to live together during the early years of the king's "Great Matter". Anne Boleyn remained nominally in the queen's household, although she was given her own fine court lodgings in late 1528. By that time it was noted by Eustace Chapuys (Imperial Ambassador to England from the Duchy of Savoy) (c.1490 –1556) that "greater court is now paid to her every day than has been to the queen for a long time". However, she was still not queen and Anne was furious to discover that the king dined on occasion with his wife and allowed her to make his shirts.

Anne Boleyn had a fiery temper and was not always easy to live with. In November 1530 she and Henry had a public argument. Chapuys reported that Anne was weeping and lamenting the loss of her honour and "threatening the king that she would leave him". The possibility of losing his great love caused Henry to burst into tears. They soon reconciled, but even the besotted monarch was heard to complain that Anne was "not like the Queen, who have never in her life used ill words to him," according to Chapuys.

Henry's court must have been a tense place with both Catherine and Anne living there. To the king's anger, the queen resolutely refused to leave his side for fear that it would appear that she had abandoned him. Finally, on the morning of 11 July 1531 Henry and Anne secretly rode away from Windsor Castle, leaving Catherine behind.

When Henry had not returned after six days, Catherine sent him a message, enquiring about his health and, said Chapuys, "to tell him of the concern she felt in not having been able to speak with him at his departure". In a fury, Henry replied that she was "an obstinate woman" who had brought public shame on him by causing him to be cited to appear before a court in Rome. Undaunted, Catherine replied, receiving a response forbidding her from sending him any messages or gifts in future. Catherine lived for another four-and-a-half years, but she never saw Henry again.

WILLIAM TYNDALE (C.1494–1536)

Anne Boleyn was well known for her interest in religious reform, which focused on her desire for the scriptures to be read in English. She was not alone in this. William Tyndale, who was born in the 1490s, was a scholar and learned in Greek and Hebrew. He spent years working on a translation of the Bible into English, finally printing his New Testament in Germany in 1525.

Henry VIII banned Tyndale's translation, though copies were smuggled into England secretly. To the established church, the idea of the laity reading the scriptures was dangerous. Tyndale's book was burned in England, but he was determined to continue, and began work on his translation of the Old Testament. He was unable to complete it, however, and was executed near Brussels in October 1536 for heresy.

Tyndale's last words were "Lord, open the King of England's eyes!". As it happened, his work, *The Obedience of a Christian Man*, had already by then been influential in Henry's decision to abandon the pope. Within a few years of his death, the king had ordered an official English Bible to be produced, which was based heavily on Tyndale's own work.

SUPREME HEAD OF THE CHURCH OF ENGLAND

With the failure of the Blackfriars trial, it became apparent to Henry that his chance of securing a papal annulment was remote. Encouraged by Anne Boleyn, he began to turn towards more radical solutions.

Anne, who was interested in religious reform, possessed a number of anti-clerical works, including Simon Fish's *The Supplication of Beggars*, which argued that the king's laws could not be enforced against the pope's since the chancellor was usually a priest. Anne liked to mark out relevant passages in such books and bring them to Henry's attention; in time the more conservative-minded king gradually came round to her way of thinking.

In 1530, Henry took his first step against the papacy by prosecuting 15 clerics and one lay proctor for prioritizing papal law over that of the king – the offence of praemunire. In January 1531, when the entire clergy met in convocation, they were ordered to purchase a royal pardon for praemunire for £100,000. After some debate, this was agreed on 24 January. Henry was not finished with the clergy, sending them a document containing five articles on 7 February. The first, and most significant, required that they recognize him as Sole Protector and Supreme Head of the Church in England.

After some debate a compromise was reached on 11 February 1531, with the clergy agreeing to acknowledge the king as "Supreme Head of the Church of England, as far as the law of Christ allows". The qualification to the title effectively made it meaningless but, for Henry, the assumption of the role of Supreme Head of the Church was the first step towards breaking with Rome. It effectively made him "Pope in England".

Following the praemunire manoeuvres of early 1531, Henry became increasingly anti-papal in outlook, and attempted to goad the pope into granting his annulment. In early 1532, for example, he passed the Act for the Conditional Restraint of Annates, which stopped the highly lucrative payment of bishop's revenues being passed to Rome.

For Henry VIII, the decisive moment came in August 1532 with the death of the conservative William Warham, Archbishop of Canterbury. This allowed the appointment of a more reform-minded candidate, Thomas Cranmer (1489–1556), who had been a chaplain to Anne Boleyn's father. Like Anne herself, there were many who suspected Cranmer of being a "heretic". He did, indeed, hold reformist views and was secretly married.

Pope Clement VII may have had private doubts about Cranmer's suitability but, anxious to appease the English king, he dispatched the documents confirming the appointment in March

1533. As soon as they arrived, the new archbishop repudiated his oath of loyalty to the pope, breaking the English church from Rome, with Henry as its Supreme Head.

Henry VIII always considered himself a Catholic and continued to arrest and execute Protestants up until the end of his reign, with his own sixth wife, Catherine Parr, narrowly avoiding imprisonment for heresy in the 1540s. However, the break with Rome and the other religious changes that he introduced placed England firmly on the road to Protestantism. More immediately, it also meant that the pope no longer had the authority to rule in his divorce. In May 1533, Cranmer held a church court to pronounce Henry VIII's first marriage void. He then hurried back to London to crown the new Queen of England: Anne Boleyn.

SIR THOMAS MORE (1478–1535)

Cardinal Wolsey was not the only prominent figure to fall during Henry VIII's request for a divorce. Sir Thomas More, who was a lawyer, was one of the most renowned humanist scholars of his day. He succeeded Wolsey as Lord Chancellor, but his conscience was troubled. He was unable to accept that Henry was Supreme Head of the Church of England or the king's divorce, something which led to his imprisonment. He was executed in 1535.

6

THE SIX WIVES OF HENRY VIII

No king of England was as much married as Henry VIII, with the popular rhyme "Divorced, Beheaded, Died, Divorced, Beheaded, Survived" recording their unenviable fates. His first marriage finally ended in an annulment in 1533, which allowed him to marry Anne Boleyn.

ANNE BOLEYN'S CORONATION

Only two of Henry VIII's wives were crowned. Catherine of Aragon shared his coronation at the beginning of the reign, while Anne Boleyn was crowned alone at the end of May 1533.

Anne had married the king in a secret ceremony on 25 January 1533 when she was in the early stages of pregnancy. It was imperative that the king secure the annulment of his first marriage; this he did with his new Archbishop of Canterbury, Thomas Cranmer, holding an ecclesiastical court at Dunstable, before he rushed back south to crown the new queen.

The festivities began on Thursday 29 May, with Anne taking to her barge at Greenwich to go by water to the Tower of London. The river pageant was a great sight, with boats decked out in steamers and banners displaying the badges of the guilds of London going before her, while minstrels played as they sailed.

She was not entirely happy with her reception: the Imperial Ambassador, Eustace Chapuys, considered that the ceremony was "altogether a cold, poor, and most unpleasing sight". Another account stated that, when the people saw the banners displaying Henry and Anne's initials, they cried out "HA!" mockingly. In the main, however, the crowds that flocked to watch the festivities were positive, causing Anne to "rejoice".

Henry was waiting for his wife when she landed at the Tower, greeting her with what Hall described as "a noble loving countenance". The following day was spent at the Tower, where the king dubbed 19 Knights of the Bath – a ceremony traditionally held in the days leading up to a monarch's coronation. Anne, who was nearly six months pregnant, spent the day resting.

The next day a procession set out on horseback from the Tower, headed by the foreign ambassadors, riding in pairs. Then came esquires and knights, before lower members of the nobility and the new Knights of the Bath dressed in violet edged with ermine. Other dignitaries followed, before the queen herself, carried in a fine litter under a canopy. Next came her ladies, either riding or in coaches. As they travelled through the streets, they passed pageants extolling the new queen's virtues.

Anne spent the night at Westminster, before assembling with her ladies and much of the nobility at 8 am on Sunday 1 June. They walked in procession to Westminster Abbey where Anne was crowned as Queen of England by the Archbishop of Canterbury. The coronation of Anne Boleyn was the last great ceremonial occasion of Henry's reign and was designed to demonstrate the legitimacy of the king's new marriage, as well as enhancing Anne's status. As it turned out, within three years of her coronation the new queen would be dead.

LIKE BROTHER, LIKE SISTERS

Henry VIII was not the only member of his family to suffer marital troubles. His elder sister, Margaret, was widowed when her husband, James IV, was killed in battle against the English in 1513. She next married Archibald Douglas, Earl of Angus (1489–1557), but the marriage was far from happy. In October 1518, she asked her brother to arrange her divorce, something which he refused to countenance since it would bring the legitimacy of her daughter, Margaret Douglas (1515–1578), into question. Margaret persisted, however, at one point turning the guns of her castle on her husband when Henry sent him back to Scotland. The marriage was finally annulled in February 1527.

Margaret Tudor had not finished with marriage and, early the following year, she took the younger Henry Stewart (1495–1552) as her third husband. Like her second marriage, the relationship was troubled, although she was thwarted in her attempts to secure a divorce by her son, James V, who feared that she would take Angus back.

Margaret was not the only one of Henry VIII's sisters to have a complicated marital career. His younger sister, Mary (1496–1533), was married to Louis XII of France (1498–1515) in 1514.

When he died only weeks later, she secretly wed her brother's best friend, Charles Brandon (1484–1545), Duke of Suffolk, who had journeyed to France to bring her home.

Suffolk had previously become engaged to a lady named Anne Browne, before abandoning her when she was pregnant to marry her aunt, Margaret Mortimer. He was later forced to return to Anne, who had died by the time of his marriage to Mary. In spite of this, when he took the French queen as his wife he was engaged to another lady, Elizabeth Grey. Given this, it was thought prudent by Mary and Suffolk to secure a papal dispensation for their marriage, which arrived – somewhat belatedly – in 1528.

CATHERINE OF ARAGON'S LAST LETTER

Following her separation from Henry, Catherine of Aragon spent years moving from one uncomfortable residence to another at the king's command. In December 1535 she was at Kimbolton in Cambridgeshire when she fell dangerously ill.

In the early hours of 7 January 1536 Catherine, who knew she was dying, composed a last letter to "My most dear lord, king and husband". She stated that she pardoned him for his offences, hoping "to put you in remembrance with a few words of the health and safeguard of your soul which you ought to prefer before all worldly matters, and before the care and pampering of your body, for the which you have cast me into many calamities and yourself into many troubles". After asking him to be a good father to her daughter and to provide dowries for her three maids, she ended "Lastly, I make this vow, that mine eyes desire you above all things".

Catherine died later that day. Henry, who Chapuys described as "like one transported with joy", marked the occasion by wearing celebratory yellow when they received word of her death. Anne Boleyn also celebrated, although her husband had already begun a relationship with the woman who would become his third wife.

THE EXECUTION OF ANNE BOLEYN

Henry's infatuation with Anne Boleyn did not long survive their marriage. He took a mistress in the summer of 1533 and another the following year, before turning his attention to one of Anne's maids, Jane Seymour (1508–1537). On the day of Catherine of Aragon's funeral – 29 January 1536 – Anne, who had thus far only produced a daughter (Princess, later Queen, Elizabeth 1533–1603), miscarried a son. This was a terrible disaster for the queen, with Henry declaring that he had been bewitched and that he could see that "he would have no more boys by her".

On the night of 30 April 1536, a young musician in Anne's employment named Mark Smeaton (c.1512–1536) went to dine with the king's chief minister, Thomas Cromwell. Only a few weeks before, Anne had quarrelled with the minister, declaring that she would have his head. Instead, Cromwell, who had allied himself with the Seymours and Princess Mary, was determined to have hers. Smeaton was arrested upon his arrival and tortured. He soon confessed to having committed adultery with Anne Boleyn.

The following day the court assembled to watch the May Day jousts at Greenwich. Anne, like the rest of the court, was stunned when Henry suddenly rose to his feet and stalked away, taking only a few men with him as he rode to Westminster. Throughout the journey he questioned one of his attendants, Henry Norris (c.1482–1536), promising him a pardon if he would only confess a sin. Norris said nothing and, the following morning, he was sent to the Tower of London.

Anne spent an uncomfortable night at Greenwich. Although she is unlikely to have noticed the lowly Smeaton's absence, she was concerned by the king's strange conduct. The following morning several members of the royal council arrived to question her on suspicion of adultery. At 5 pm she was taken by water to the Tower, a place from which she would never emerge.

On her arrival, the queen's self-composure gave way and she fell to her knees "beseeching God to help her as she was not guilty of her accusement". As she entered, she asked her gaoler, Sir William Kingston, who was the lieutenant of the Tower, "Shall I go in a dungeon?", before being assured that she would be lodged in the royal apartments. She was attended by only four ladies who reported her words and conduct to Thomas Cromwell.

By the time that she arrived at the Tower, Anne was aware that she had been accused of adultery with Smeaton and Norris, as well as incest with her brother, George, who was also arrested. Crying out that Norris and Smeaton had accused her, she asked Kingston "Shall I die without justice?" When the lieutenant assured her that "The poorest subject of the king hath had justice", she laughed.

On 12 May 1536, Norris and Smeaton, along with two other men of the court – Francis Weston (c.1511–1536) and William Brereton (c.1487–1536) – were tried for treason at Westminster Hall. Unsurprisingly, they were found guilty, with the verdict making Anne's own trial on 15 May a foregone conclusion. Although the queen defended herself eloquently, she was convicted, and sentenced to be burned or beheaded at the king's pleasure. Immediately after her trial, her brother was also tried and convicted.

Anne's five "lovers" were executed together on 17 May, with all but Smeaton continuing to declare their innocence – strong evidence that the charges were trumped up in order to allow the king to marry again. Similarly, Anne swore her innocence on the sacrament in front of Sir William Kingston. The night before her death, she was in good spirits, declaring that her nickname would be "Queen Anne Lack-Head".

On the morning of 19 May she stepped out of the royal apartments and made her way to Tower Green where a crowd had assembled. After mounting a scaffold, she made a short speech before kneeling on the straw. As a small act of mercy, Henry had sent to Calais for a swordsman to behead his wife, rather than entrusting her death to a clumsy axe. As she prayed, the swordsman stepped up behind her and decapitated her with one blow. Her lips and eyes continued to move in prayer as the head fell to the ground.

CARING FOR THE QUEEN

Tudor queens, like kings, required a household of attendants to care for them. A queen was attended by her ladies-in-waiting, who acted both as companions and as servants, although they were often of very high rank. The queen's "great ladies", who were drawn from the duchesses and countesses in England, played a largely ceremonial role at state occasions.

After the great ladies, there were the ladies of the privy chamber, who tended to the queen's daily needs. These were usually the wives of minor peers or the married daughters of high-ranking noblemen. Finally, the queen employed maids of honour, who were unmarried girls of at least 12-years-old and born of good family.

Maids of honour were educated in the queen's household. Like the higher-ranking ladies-in-waiting, they were also expected to carry out menial tasks. The Marchioness of Exeter, for example, held the basin for Jane Seymour to wash her hands in before she ate. These roles were highly sought after since they allowed the women to be physically close to the queen.

For unmarried girls, being at court gave them access to potential husbands. Three of Henry VIII's English wives first caught his eye while they were serving as maids of honour.

GABLE HOODS VS FRENCH CAPS

During the reign of Henry VIII, his wives' clothing came to take on a surprising political significance. Anne Boleyn was well known for favouring the fashionable and daring French hood. At a time when women were expected to keep their hair covered, this jewelled cap, which allowed for the front part of the hair to be displayed, was revolutionary. It suited Anne Boleyn's outspoken personality that she chose to wear the hood at court.

Anne's successor, Jane Seymour, first came to the king's attention late in 1535. She was the eldest daughter of Sir John Seymour (c.1474–1536) of Wolf Hall in Wiltshire and his wife, Margery Wentworth (c.1478–1550), who was a cousin of Anne Boleyn's mother and related to the powerful Howard family. These connections allowed Jane to take up a post in the household first of Catherine of Aragon and, later, of Anne Boleyn. Jane was, according to Chapuys,"not a woman of great wit" nor a beauty. However, she presented an air of quiet virtue, which attracted the king. When, early in 1536, Henry sent her a letter with a purse of gold, she impressed him by refusing to accept either. Instead, she declared "that she had no greater riches in the world than her honour, which she would not injure for a thousand deaths". Following this, Henry abandoned attempts to make Jane his mistress, instead viewing her as a potential bride. She appeared to him as the exact opposite of the fiery and worldly Anne Boleyn.

Jane and Henry were betrothed the day after Anne Boleyn's execution and married less than two weeks later. Jane, who adopted the motto Bound to Obey and Serve, presented herself as a model of quiet virtue. She deliberately depicted herself as a contrast to Anne and, as part of this, wore an unflattering English Gable Hood, which was shaped like the pitched roof of a house and entirely covered the hair. Jane made a point of wearing the traditional headwear as part of her image as a virtuous and pious woman.

Given that she and her predecessor had risen from the queen's household, it is no surprise that Jane determined that her maids wear the garment as well. When she appointed the French-educated Anne Basset (1521–c.1558) as her maid in September 1537, the queen insisted that the girl replace all her hoods, even though the new gable hoods "became her nothing so well as the French hood". For Jane, this was exactly the point – she wanted no rivals in her household.

Henry VIII never permitted Jane to take a political role, publicly reminding her of Anne Boleyn's fate in late 1536 when she attempted to speak out against the Dissolution of the Monasteries. Until she provided an heir she knew that her position was far from secure, with her coronation pointedly postponed by the king. Finally, on 12 October 1537, after a long labour, Jane gave birth to a son – Edward (later Edward VI, 1537–1553). As England erupted in celebration, Jane was well enough to send out letters announcing the birth and to make an appearance at the christening. However, by 16 October 1536, she had contracted childbed fever. She died on 24 October 1537, only 12 days after the birth of her son. Her maids, clad in their gable hoods, accompanied the queen's body to its burial at Windsor. Jane's successor as queen, Anne of Cleves (1515–1557), did not follow the former queen's dress sense. She later attempted to make herself more pleasing to Henry by adopting the comely French hood.

A COURT OUTING

Jane Seymour's sudden death left Henry VIII without a new candidate for a bride. He kept many of Jane Seymour's ladies at court following her death. Two, in particular, caught his attention, leading to rumours that either Mary Shelton (1510–1571) or Margaret Skipwith (1520–1583) would become his next wife. In August 1539, he invited the ladies of the queen's privy chamber to travel down to Portsmouth to view the ships of the navy, including the newly refurbished *Mary Rose* and the *Great Harry* (or *Henry Grace a Dieu*). Henry was proud of his fleet, and the ladies politely informed him that they were "things so goodly to behold that in our lives we have not seen (excepting your royal person and my lord the Prince your son) a more pleasant sight". There were gifts waiting for the ladies aboard the king's "new great ship" (which was, perhaps, the *Great Harry*), along with music and entertainments.

Henry made some futile attempts to make a French or Imperial match, after which he considered the German duchy of Cleves. Although Catholic, Cleves was allied to the Protestant Schmalkaldic League which, like Henry, was in dispute with the Holy Roman emperor, Charles V. Conveniently, the Duke of Cleves, had two unmarried sisters: Anne and Amelia (1517–1586). After commissioning portraits of the pair, Henry selected the elder sister.

A FLANDERS MARE

Anne of Cleves (1515–1557) arrived in England in December 1539 and made her way towards London. Although it was not planned that he should meet her before her official reception at Greenwich, Henry was too excited to wait. He resolved to visit Anne, disguised as a messenger, on New Year's Eve. This was part of the chivalric tradition of courtly love and it was expected by the king that, when he came upon his fiancé at Rochester Castle, she would immediately recognize him and throw herself into his arms.

Unfortunately, Anne was watching a bull baiting out of her window and ignored the overweight and aged stranger who arrived bearing the king's New Year's presents. Undaunted, Henry embraced her but Anne, who must have been alarmed at the messenger's over-familiarity, continued to studiously look out the window. Admitting defeat, Henry stalked out of the chamber, only to re-emerge wearing a purple velvet coat. This was the signal that those in attendance could recognize him and they immediately fell to their knees. Anne also finally realized that it was Henry and the couple spent the evening together, talking through interpreters.

As soon as the tide changed the following day, Henry left for London, complaining to his attendants that "I see nothing in this woman as men report of her; and I marvel that wise men would make such report as they have done". Although he probably did not, as later claimed, insist that a Flanders mare had been sent instead of a woman, it is clear that he found Anne unattractive.

Henry was unable to break his engagement and the couple married on 6 January 1540. All attempts to consummate the match failed, with the king complaining that he doubted Anne's virginity and that she smelled. Finally, in July 1540, when he had already begun a relationship with Catherine Howard – the maid of honour who would become his fifth wife – he annulled the match, declaring Anne to be "his sister".

A TUDOR WEDDING

Henry VIII's weddings were usually conducted quietly, with only a few witnesses. Weddings in the Tudor period could, however, be lavish affairs. A marriage settlement dated 15 May 1528 survives, outlining the agreement made between a widower, William Reed of Weybridge in Surrey and his prospective father-in-law, John Blount. In the agreement, Reed covenanted to marry Blount's daughter, Isabel, by 10 June at the latest. This left little time to arrange the wedding, which was to be celebrated with a feast afterwards.

Marriage settlements were designed to provide for the woman in her widowhood, with the financial provision called a "dower". Since married women could hold no property, it was essential that their income be confirmed before they were wed. In Reed's settlement, he promised to pass estates worth more than £30 a year to trustees, in order to ensure that the income was made available to Isabel and her children after his decease.

In return for this dower, John Blount agreed to make a marriage payment – or dowry – of 400 marks in instalments. This was a substantial sum and demonstrates the eagerness of the bride's father to arrange the marriage.

A MUCH-MARRIED QUEEN

After the execution of Catherine Howard (see pages 90–92) for adultery in February 1542, unsurprisingly Henry found it difficult to obtain a sixth bride. He eventually chose Catherine Parr (1512–1548), a woman who bears the distinction of being the most-married English queen.

Catherine had already been widowed twice when she caught the king's attention early in 1543. She was far from eager for the match, having already decided to marry Sir Thomas Seymour (1508–1549), the brother of Henry's third wife. In the event, she proved to be a successful queen, serving as regent when Henry invaded France and bringing the royal children back to court. She remained in love with Thomas Seymour, however, and in May 1547, only a few months after Henry's death, she wed her dashing suitor in secret.

Catherine's fourth marriage, which was her only love match, proved to be a disaster. It alienated her from the court of her stepson, Edward VI, as well as causing a rift with her young stepdaughter, Princess Elizabeth, whom the queen caught embracing her husband. On 30 August 1548, Catherine Parr, the wife who survived marriage to Henry VIII, gave birth to her only child. She failed to recover, dying delirious and railing against her husband six days later.

7

TREASON

Henry VIII was acutely conscious of the circumstances of his father's rise to the throne and the political instability of the Wars of the Roses. He was determined to preserve his dynasty and position at all costs, a determination that led to him being remembered by many as a tyrant.

THE PILGRIMAGE OF GRACE

Although Henry always considered himself to be a Catholic, he embraced his position as Supreme Head of the Church of England and, in the 1530s, set in place a series of reforms. A major feature of this was the Dissolution of the Monasteries. This began after Thomas Cromwell, who had been appointed as vicar general of England, instituted visitations to the religious houses of England.

Their reports were often damning. It was in Henry and Cromwell's interests that these reports should make lurid reading (the abbot of Bury St Edmunds, for example, was found to delight in playing at dice and cards, as well as permitting women to frequent his monastery), since they were used as the basis for dissolving the religious houses in England and appropriating their substantial wealth.

At Easter in 1536, as a first step, the king was granted control over all the smaller monasteries by Parliament, and immediately set about dissolving them. He turned his attention to the larger houses in 1539.

The Dissolution of the Monasteries was greeted by murmurings of discontent. By the autumn of 1536, the country was awash with rumours. Nicholas Melton, who was a cobbler in Louth in Lincolnshire, for example, had heard that the king meant to confiscate all the jewels and ornaments of the parish churches – a not too surprising assumption given what was then happening in the monasteries.

On 1 October 1536, the vicar of Louth denounced the religious changes from his pulpit. Following the service, the townspeople assembled outside the church to walk in procession behind their three silver crosses. As they readied themselves, a yeoman named Thomas Foster declared loudly "Go we to follow the crosses for and if they be taken from us we be like to follow them no more". As resentment bubbled, Nicholas Melton, who adopted the alias of "Captain Cobbler", took charge. The next morning the townsmen met again to ring the bells in alarm.

The events at Louth raised most of Lincolnshire into rebellion against the king and his religious polices. By 6 October, 40,000 men had gathered at Lincoln under the banner of the five wounds of Christ. At Windsor, the king began to order military preparations, but the size of the uprising was unprecedented. Although he never wavered in his fury at the rebels, not everyone at court was convinced by the righteousness of his position. Even the then queen, meek Jane Seymour, attempted to intervene, arguing that the uprising was God's judgment for the attacks on the monasteries.

The rebels' demands were long and included the request that the church be able to retain its ancient liberties and that no more abbeys be suppressed. Henry was bullish in response, writing to the rebels, whom he considered to be "the rude commons of one shire, and that one of the most brute and beastly of the whole realm". His refusal to accept any of the demands, coupled with the Lincolnshire uprising's poor leadership meant that it soon dispersed. However, before they did so, Yorkshire had also begun to rise in support.

The Yorkshire rebellion enjoyed a more effective leadership under the command of Robert Aske (1500–1537), a well-connected and intelligent lawyer. Aske and his supporters considered their actions akin to a religious crusade, or a "pilgrimage of grace", carrying crosses and religious banners as they gathered support. By 14 October, the whole of Yorkshire was in arms, although the rebels were careful to express their loyalty to the king – provided that he changed his policies.

In reality, the 40,000 well-ordered men who assembled at Doncaster on 26 October threatened Henry's throne. In the face of this opposition, Henry was forced to agree a truce with the rebels and sign a general pardon. He showed a remarkable ability to dissimulate, even inviting Aske to court that Christmas as his guest. As the rebels began to return home, however, he struck. A further insurrection led by Sir Francis Bigod (1507–1537) in February 1537 gave Henry the excuse he needed to repudiate the rebels' pardon and order the leaders' arrests. Many of the leading rebels, including Aske himself, were executed the following year. Henry VIII would accept no opposition to his rule. By early 1540 there were no religious houses left in England, with their lands, buildings and wealth largely in the hands of the king. His throne also remained secure for the remainder of his reign.

ACTS OF ATTAINDER

Since medieval times, Parliament had sometimes passed Acts of Attainder, which legally condemned an individual for a crime without the need for a trial. Such Attainders could confiscate the condemned's property, as well as frequently sentencing them to death. Although the process existed long before the 16th century, the Tudors increased the use of Attainders. Those accused of treason in Tudor England were not always granted the luxury of a trial. On her arrival at the Tower of London, Anne Boleyn had asked whether she would die without justice and, while the result of her trial was largely a foregone conclusion, she was at least given an opportunity to defend herself. Her brother, who was tried immediately after her, presented himself so well that Chapuys remarked "that many who were present at the trial, and heard what he said, had no difficulty in waging two-to-one that he would be acquitted".

As Henry's reign went on, he began to use Acts of Attainder in high-profile cases, removing the need for a trial. Instead, the Attainder enacted into law that the accused was guilty of treason, allowing their property to be confiscated and their execution to be arranged. Acts of Attainder meant that some members of the court, such as Queen Catherine Howard and Thomas Cromwell, went to their deaths without even the pretence of justice or a chance to defend themselves.

THE DEATH OF THOMAS CROMWELL (1485–1540)

Thomas Cromwell, the low-born son of a Putney blacksmith, rose in the king's service to become his chief minister and he was the architect of many royal policies, including the Dissolution of the Monasteries. However, he incurred the king's displeasure when he arranged his marriage to Anne of Cleves. Henry found Anne physically unattractive and blamed Cromwell, who had recommended the match.

On 10 June 1540, when the minister went to sit in his usual place at a council meeting, the Duke of Norfolk called out "Cromwell, do not sit there; that is no place for thee. Traitors do not sit among gentlemen". As he declared angrily "I am not a traitor", guards entered to take him to the Tower.

Cromwell was denied a trial, instead being convicted of treason in an Act of Attainder. Even then, Henry was determined to make use of his former minister, sending word that he should give a full account of everything that had happened since Anne of Cleves arrived in England, in the hope that it would assist him in obtaining a divorce. Cromwell duly wrote an account, declaring that he was Henry's "most lamentable servant and prisoner prostrate at the feet of your most excellent majesty". This did not save him and he went to the block on 28 July 1540, beheaded "by a ragged and butcherly miser, who very ungodly performed the office".

TUDOR BANKRUPTCY

The Attainders against Tudor traitors stripped them of their property, and passed everything that they owned to the Crown. In 1542, Parliament passed a piece of legislation that also dealt with secular goods, although in a civil rather than criminal law context. The 1542 Statute of Bankrupts was the first time that the concept of bankruptcy passed into English law. The Statute ensured that creditors could act to seize the goods of debtors, providing a remedy that ensured that debtors could not simply flee the country without paying what was owed. The Statute remained in force until the nineteenth century and was intended to ensure that people "craftily obtaining into their hands great substance of other men's goods" would no longer be able to avoid paying them back. It was the first time that the word "Bankrupt" was used in English law, with the Statute laying the foundation for all later legislation on the subject.

THE BEHEADING OF CATHERINE HOWARD

When Henry VIII offered to make the widowed Duchess of Milan his fourth wife in 1538, she reportedly replied that "she had but one head, if she had two, one should be at his Majesty's service". Anne Boleyn's execution damaged Henry's reputation as a husband, but it did not stop Anne's first cousin, the teenaged Catherine Howard, from becoming his fifth wife in July 1540.

To Henry, Catherine was young, beautiful and pure, but she was also a girl with a past. On 2 November 1542, after the court had returned from a northern progress, Archbishop Cranmer passed the king a note stating that he had received intelligence about the queen's activities before her marriage.

Catherine had been raised in the household of her father's step-mother, the dowager Duchess of Norfolk and was remembered by Mary Lascelles who had been in the household, as being "light both in living and condition". Following investigations into her childhood, it was confirmed that she had begun a youthful relationship with Henry Mannox, a lowly music tutor. He confessed that, although they had stopped short of sexual intercourse, he knew the secret parts of her body well.

Once she had tired of Mannox, the young Catherine had begun an affair with Francis Dereham, a gentleman of the household. The couple were so often together that even Catherine's step-grandmother heard of the relationship, commenting fondly when Dereham was sought that "I warrant you if you seek him in Catherine Howard's chamber you shall find him there". Both Catherine and Dereham, under interrogation, admitted to a sexual relationship although the queen, unlike her former lover, refused to agree that she had been formally betrothed. Such a promise would have made her marriage to the king invalid and was the only means by which she could have hoped to save her life.

Henry had originally refused to believe the accusations levelled against Catherine, but as the truth emerged, he called for a sword to slay her himself. On 4 November, as his wife practised her dance steps at Hampton Court, guards burst into her chamber, telling her bluntly that "it is no more time to dance". A week later she was sent as a prisoner to Syon House.

While failing to inform the king of her conduct before her marriage was dangerous, worse was to emerge during the investigation. When she had first arrived at court, Catherine had made the acquaintance of Thomas Culpeper (1514–1541), a handsome young man of the king's privy chamber. By 1540 Henry VIII was a very poor physical specimen, grossly overweight and incapacitated by an ulcerated leg. He presented a poor contrast to Culpeper, to whom Catherine wrote lovingly, confiding that "I never longed so much for [a] thing as I do to see you and to speak with you".

Although they both denied it, the pair were almost certainly lovers, with the queen's lady-in-waiting, Lady Rochford, seeking out back doors to the queen's apartments at every house that the royal couple stayed in on the northern progress. The couple would meet at night with only Lady Rochford present, who would tactfully turn her back or even fall asleep. This was certainly treason owing to the possibility that Catherine might conceive a "royal" child from the encounters.

Dereham and Culpeper were executed on 10 December 1541. Catherine remained a prisoner, but no one expected her to live. On 16 January 1542 Parliament opened in London and condemned both the queen and Lady Rochford without trial. On 10 February 1542, Catherine was taken by water to the Tower of London. Two days later, she was informed that she would die the next morning, and she spent her last evening practising with the executioner's block to ensure that she died with dignity. The following morning she mounted a scaffold on Tower Green to become the second of Henry's wives to be beheaded.

METHODS OF EXECUTION

There were a range of possible execution methods in Tudor England. In April 1531, Bishop Fisher's cook, who had confessed to trying to poison his employer, was boiled to death – a common sentence for poisoning. Heretics were often burned at the stake. For treason, the sentence was usually for the person to be hanged, drawn and quartered.

The Duke of Buckingham was tried for treason in 1521. After his conviction, the sentence against him was set out horrific detail, ordering him to be "led to the king's prison, and there laid on a hurdle, and so drawn to the place of execution, and there be hanged, cut down alive; your members be cut off, and cast into the fire; your bowels burnt before you; your head smitten off, and your body quartered and divided at the king's will".

Such deaths were designed to humiliate convicted traitors, as well as draw out the agony as much as possible. They were common, although for higher status prisoners, such as the Duke of Buckingham, the sentence was usually commuted by the king to beheading with an axe. Even this could be far from merciful. An inexperienced headsman was used to execute the 70-year-old Countess of Salisbury in 1541, and so botched the job that it took ten blows of the axe before he was able to sever her head.

HENRY HOWARD, EARL OF SURREY (1517–1547)

Executions for treason continued right up to Henry VIII's death; on 19 January 1547, only nine days before the old king died, Henry Howard, Earl of Surrey, was beheaded.

On 12 December 1546, the Earl and his father, the aged Duke of Norfolk (1473–1554), were suddenly arrested and sent to the Tower. It was Surrey who was the direct focus of the investigation, amid claims that he had assumed the royal arms of Edward the Confessor, a prerogative that belonged only to the king and the Prince of Wales. He was also reported to have said "if God should call the king to his mercy, who were so meet to govern the Prince as my lord his father [Norfolk]?"

Henry, who was already unwell, had concerns that Surrey had designs on the regency when his nine-year-old son Edward became king or, worse, wanted to become monarch himself. In 1547 this was not so far-fetched, given the fact that the last boy king, Edward V, who was Henry VIII's own uncle, had been deposed and probably murdered 60 years before. Surrey also had a very strong claim to the throne through his mother.

For the dying Henry VIII, Surrey and Norfolk were threats to his son. He made handwritten amendments to the document listing the charges against the pair, personally ordering Surrey's death. The earl was unfortunate, but his father, who was also sentenced to die, survived the king and was finally released by Queen Mary in 1553.

8

A BOY KING AND A GIRL QUEEN

Edward VI: Born 12 October 1537; Died 6 July 1553
Reigned 28 January 1547–6 July 1553
Lady Jane Grey, Nine Days Queen:
Born October 1537; Died 12 February 1554
Reigned 10 July 1553–19 July 1553
Mary I: Born 18 February 1516; Died 17 November 1558
Reigned 19 July 1553–17 November 1558

Henry VIII died on 28 January 1547 after nearly 40 years on the throne. His heir was his son, Edward, in whom he placed his hopes for the future of his dynasty. Failing that, under the terms of both the third Act of Succession, which was passed in 1545, and Henry's own will, the crown was to pass to Princesses Mary and Elizabeth in turn. If none of Henry's children had issue, then the throne would pass to the heirs of his younger sister Mary.

A PRECOCIOUS KING

Henry VIII's much-longed-for son, Edward VI, was nine years old when he came to the throne. He was a small, pale child who resembled his mother. From the age of six, the boy had been subject to a rigorous educational regime, designed to produce a Renaissance monarch. His accession was greeted with considerable hope, with his tutor, John Cheke, writing in 1553 that "with the lord's blessing, he will prove such a king, as neither yield to Josiah in the maintenance of true religion, nor to Solomon in the management of the state, nor to David in the encouragement of godliness".

Edward was an ardent Protestant and had a firm sense of his responsibilities as king and as head of the royal family. He was particularly concerned about the conduct of his 30-year-old half-sister, writing to his stepmother when he was only eight-years-old to ask her to "preserve, therefore, I pray you, my dear sister Mary from all the wiles and enchantments of the evil one, and beseech her to attend no longer to foreign dances and merriments which do not become a most Christian princess". Shortly after he became king he attempted to arrange Mary a marriage in order to "change her opinions".

Edward grew into a clever but cold young man. He showed a business-like efficiency in the negotiations for his proposed marriage with Elizabeth of France in 1551, noting in his diary that she was to be "brought at her father's expense three months before she was 12, sufficiently jewelled and stuffed". He also showed no compunction in executing his two uncles or in disinheriting his half-sister, Elizabeth, of whom he appeared to be fond.

HENRY VIII'S WILL

Henry VIII updated his will before he left for war in France in 1544, for a campaign in which he had hoped to resurrect the English crown's ancient claim to France. Although in very poor health and overweight, the invasion, in which he captured Boulogne, had reinvigorated him for a time. At the end of December 1546, when the king was dying, a new will was drafted which has always been the subject of much controversy since the question of its validity was of great importance to the crown. Less than six months after Henry's death, his daughter Mary told the Spanish ambassador "quite frankly that the testament which was said to be that of the late king might or might not be genuine; she did not know". Mary's doubts lie in the fact that the document was listed as signed with a stamp, something which would cast its validity into doubt. His younger daughter Elizabeth, however, believed that it was genuine, writing in 1559 to the Dean and Chapter of Windsor to inform them that she wished to carry out one of the bequests in her father's will.

Henry VIII always hated writing and had a stamp made with his signature. This allowed documents to be executed without his presence. The disputed will has been examined several times, but it has never been conclusively proved whether or not Henry actually signed it. While there are no indentations on the parchment as would generally be expected if the stamp was used, the same applies for some other documents definitely known to have been signed with the stamp. The signatures on the will are not uniform, with a slight tremble evident in the writing, although this is also known from some documents signed with the stamp.

It is possible that, even if it was signed with a stamp, the will represented Henry's true wishes. In the document, Henry bequeathed the throne to his three children in turn. If they died without issue, instead of the crown passing to the heirs of his elder sister, Margaret, he decreed that his younger sister's children should inherit.

Of more immediate importance in 1547, he also included provision for Edward's minority, refusing to appoint a Lord Protector and, instead, naming 16 executors who were to rule England. This was an unprecedented and, in reality, unworkable arrangement. The old king's brother-in-law, Edward Seymour (1500–1552), had the will in his possession when Henry died and immediately set out to gain physical possession of the boy king, who was staying at Enfield.

Within only a few days of the death, Seymour had become Lord Protector, as well as appointing himself Duke of Somerset. As the new king's senior uncle, he was the obvious choice, although the appointment was not well received by his younger brother, Thomas Seymour.

THE ARREST OF SIR THOMAS SEYMOUR

Edward VI's younger uncle, Thomas Seymour (1508–1549), was ennobled as Baron Seymour of Sudeley in February 1547, but received no political role in the new regime. He was unable to contain his jealousy of his brother's position and married the queen dowager, Catherine Parr, in the hope of increasing his influence at court. He also secured the wardship and rights to the marriage of Henry VIII's great-niece, Lady Jane Grey, intending that she would marry the king himself. To this end, Seymour attempted to make the nine-year-old king love him, through secret gifts of pocket money.

Ultimately, Seymour's "vanity and folly" (so described by 17th century antiquary Sir William Dugdale) brought about his ruin. His wife's death in September 1548 removed a restraining influence on him. Without a royal wife, the nobleman Henry Manners (1526–1563) told Seymour that his "power was much diminished" although he still plotted against his brother.

By January 1549 it was believed that he had 10,000 men ready to fight for his cause. The circumstances of his arrest that month are far from clear. According to a report of the Imperial Ambassador, Seymour attempted to abduct the king, creeping into Edward's bedchamber one night as he slept. As he made his way to his nephew, the king's dog began barking, waking the guards, who rushed in to find the dog killed and the intruder fled. No one was in any doubt that it had been Seymour, who was denounced as "a great rascal" by the statesman Sir William Paget

(1506–1563). He had become too dangerous to the Protector to be allowed to remain at liberty. On 17 January 1549 Somerset, decided to send him to the Tower.

Even as a prisoner, Seymour remained defiant, refusing to answer any questions except in open trial. Like so many state prisoners of the period, it soon became clear that he would not be granted the privilege of defending himself. Grudgingly, he admitted that, the previous Easter, he had considered the possibility of abducting the king, believing that "a man might bring him through the Gallery to his chamber, and so to his house". Seymour would admit to nothing more but this, coupled with the evidence against him, was enough for Parliament to condemn him. His brother, the Duke of Somerset, "for natural pity's sake" asked to be excused from that session of Parliament. His nephew, the king, whom he had worked so hard to befriend, showed no such feeling, stating coldly that he desired that justice be done.

Thomas Seymour ended his life on the scaffold at Tower Hill on 20 March 1549. According to his contemporary Hugh Latimer (c.1487–1555), he "died very dangerously, irksomely, horribly", refusing to admit his guilt and, instead, beseeching the princesses, Mary and Elizabeth, to avenge his death. He at least died relatively quickly, with two strokes of the axe.

RIVAL LORD PROTECTORS

The Duke of Somerset was described in 1552 by Francis Bourgoyne in a letter to the theologian John Calvin as "all but king, but rather esteemed by everyone as the king of kings". He was a largely popular figure during his nephew's reign, although the execution of his brother was a stain on his reputation.

Edward VI, meanwhile, grew into a clever and capable young man, anxious to rule on his own behalf and he loathed his uncle for keeping him from power. One councillor, John Dudley, Earl of Warwick (1504–1553), always showed deference to him and treated him as an adult sovereign, causing the king to rely increasingly heavily on him and to respect him above all his other councillors.

In 1550, Dudley was able to secure Somerset's removal from office as Protector, although the fallen Duke was readmitted to the council the following year. Dudley, who had become Lord President of the Council and was, in effect, regent, was not prepared to countenance any political re-emergence by his rival and, finally, on 16 October 1551 Somerset was arrested for treason and sent to the Tower.

The charges were trumped up but Edward VI was unconcerned, recording dispassionately in his journal for 22 January 1552 that "the Duke of Somerset had his head cut off upon Tower Hill between eight and nine o'clock in the morning". Dudley had already been created Duke of Northumberland and remained the de facto ruler of England until Edward's death.

A PROTESTANT KING

In spite of his breach with Rome, Henry VIII always considered himself to be a Catholic. His son was fervently Protestant and intended that the religion of England should mirror his own beliefs. This was backed by Somerset, who was already known as "not very favourable to the priests, and a great enemy to the pope in Rome", according to Richard Hilles (c.1514–1587) in 1547. The Duke, together with Archbishop Cranmer, immediately set to work creating a Protestant nation by means of a series of injunctions issued soon after Edward's accession that ordered the removal of images from churches, as well as changing some of the other traditional practices.

The changes were radical. In late 1547, the Election of Bishops Act was passed, giving the king direct power to appoint new bishops for the first time. In some cities, there was a popular appetite for change, with most of the major London churches conducting their services solely in English by

May 1548. A Protestant *Book of Common Prayer* was also brought into use.

The religious changes were not widely welcomed by everyone and the king's Catholic half-sister, Princess Mary, became a focal point for the disaffected. During 1549, she was visited by two members of the council, who came to investigate her adherence to the new religious laws. Mary refused to recognize their authority, declaring that "she would have the old service until the king came of age". She was able to enlist the help of her powerful cousin, the Holy Roman Emperor, Charles V, ensuring that Somerset gave her a verbal assurance that she could follow her faith privately.

Following Somerset's fall, Northumberland was more insistent on Mary's conformity, something with which the king full-heartedly agreed, to the extent that the princess considered fleeing from England.

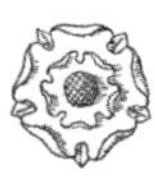

TUDOR MEDICINE

There were three distinct types of medical practitioners: physicians who diagnosed the patient and prescribed their medicine, surgeons who would operate (without anaesthetic) and an apothecary who was responsible for preparing the medicines.

In the 16th century, physicians had only a limited knowledge of illnesses and medicines, something that meant that even the most innocuous conditions could prove fatal. The young Francis II of France, for example, died of an ear infection, and given the low life expectancy of the 16th century, Henry VIII was accounted a venerable specimen by the time of his death in his mid-50s. To become a physician, it was necessary to be a university graduate, although knowledge relied heavily on Greek philosophy and the belief that ill health was caused by an imbalance in the bodily humoral fluids.

Cures could sometimes be worse than the condition. When Lord Edmund Howard (1478–1539) turned to his friend, the knowledgeable Lady Lisle (c.1493–1566), for advice when he found himself suffering from kidney stones, she kindly provided him with medicine. While the peer was grateful, confirming that "it hath done me much good, and hath caused the stone to break, so that now I void much gravel", it also had the unfortunate side-effect of causing him to "piss my bed", angering his wife, who beat him and declared that "it is children's part to bepiss their bed". The cure did little for Lord Edmund's dignity.

Very few effective drugs were known and physicians tended to prescribe treatments that caused purging, vomiting or bleeding – all cures that could, at least, had a visible effect. Some attempt was made to regulate the profession in 1512, when Parliament enacted that only those with a licence from the Bishop of London or the Dean of St Paul's would be permitted to practice medicine within seven miles of the capital. Similar measures were put in place in the rest of England, with fines payable for practising without a licence. The system was, however, largely unworkable and Tudor patients took their lives in their hands when they sought medical advice.

At Easter 1552, Edward VI fell ill with what he described as measles and smallpox. He spent the last year of his life ill, suffering considerably at the hands of Tudor doctors, as did many of his subjects. By October, he was coughing up blood, and it appeared that the 15-year-old's death was only a matter of time.

THE NINE DAYS QUEEN

Legally, Edward VI's heir was his half-sister, Mary, who was 21 years older than him and a staunch Catholic.

After Mary, the next heir was Edward's Protestant half-sister, Elizabeth. It was impossible for her to succeed before her elder half-sister and the king therefore decided to overlook her when he cast around for a new successor. The next heir was Frances Brandon, Duchess of Suffolk, who was the daughter of Henry VIII's younger sister. Frances had three daughters and the eldest, Lady Jane Grey, had conveniently married Northumber-land's son, Guildford Dudley (1535–1554) on 25 May 1553. Shortly before Edward's death on 6 July 1553, he signed a device for the succession, naming the 15-year-old Jane as heir to the throne.

Northumberland kept Edward's death a secret at first in the hope that he could apprehend Princess Mary, who had been summoned to her brother's deathbed. Unfortunately for him, Mary received word that Edward was already dead and fled into East Anglia. This was a blow for Northumberland, but only a minor one – few people seriously believed that the princess could mount a successful bid for the throne.

On 9 July 1553, Lady Jane Grey was summoned by the king's council and informed that Edward had named her as his heir. This was the first that Jane had heard of this and she fell to the ground weeping before turning to God "humbly praying and beseeching him, that if what was given to me was rightfully and lawfully mine, his divine majesty would grant me such grace and spirit that I might govern it to his glory and service, and to the advantage of the realm". She took silence as a sign of divine acceptance. The next day, the diminutive Queen Jane made her ceremonial entry to the Tower of London, wearing platform heels to ensure that she could be seen by the curious crowds.

The new queen, who was very highly educated, was as deeply committed to Protestantism as her predecessor. She was red-haired and pretty, with a freckled face. She deeply disliked both her father-in-law and her husband, informing Guildford as she tried on the royal crown that "I should be content to make my husband a duke, but would never consent to make him a king". Queen Jane meant to rule alone although, as it turned out, her authority was brief.

During the evening that Jane arrived at the Tower, a message was brought from Mary claiming the throne. The council immediately replied, refuting this on the grounds of the princess's illegitimacy. Nevertheless, her opposition was worrying and Northumberland resolved to take an army to capture her himself.

Although Jane possessed the crown and the Tower of London, she was far from popular. Few were willing to fight for Queen Jane and, as Northumberland made his way through Shoreditch, he commented that "the people press to see us, but not one sayeth God speed us". Mary, on the other hand, who had made her base at Framlingham Castle in Suffolk, found that she soon had a sizeable force of troops at her disposal.

By the time that Northumberland left London, Mary had been proclaimed queen in Buckinghamshire and Norfolk. Shortly afterwards, the crews of six royal ships that were anchored off Yarmouth mutinied in her favour. As his army slipped away, Northumberland fled to Cambridge. He was in the university town on 19 July when he heard that Mary had been proclaimed queen in London. Admitting defeat, he proclaimed her himself in the marketplace, bringing the nine-day reign of Queen Jane to an end.

At the same time, in London, Jane's own father tore down the royal canopy above her head, before fleeing the Tower. There was to be no escape for Jane, who was moved that night from the royal apartments to the prison.

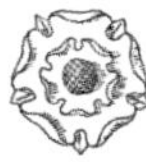

THE EXECUTION OF LADY JANE GREY

At 10 am on the morning of 12 February 1554, Guildford Dudley was led out to the scaffold on Tower Hill, where he was beheaded. The boy, although vain and spoiled, had committed no crime. His wife, Lady Jane Grey, watched from her window as his body was carried back to the chapel.

It was now Jane's turn to die; the Lieutenant of the Tower, with whom she had shared cheerful dinners in the months leading up to her death, took her out onto Tower Green. Dressed in black, she was accompanied by two gentlewomen and prayed from a book as she mounted the scaffold. The former queen kept her composure as she made a short speech, declaring that, although she had sinned against the queen, everything had been done in her name and not by her consent, allowing her to declare that "I do wash my hands thereof in innocency". She then recited a psalm before handing her gloves and handkerchief to one of her ladies, and her book to the lieutenant's brother.

As Jane took off her outer gown, the executioner went to help her, causing her to shrink back in alarm. Her ladies assisted her instead, tying a scarf around her eyes, with Jane anxiously asking the headsman whether he meant to take her head off before she knelt. Blindfolded, Jane fumbled for the block on the straw of the scaffold, crying out "What shall I do? Where is it?" A bystander helped her find it, with the girl declaring "Lord, into thy hands I commend my spirit!" before her head was severed with one stroke of the axe.

No one in England seriously believed that the 16-year-old deserved to die. The execution of Lady Jane Grey, to whom she had previously promised mercy, cast a stain over the reign of Mary Tudor.

9

BLOODY MARY

Mary I swept to the throne on a wave of popular support but, just over five years later, bonfires were lit in the streets of London to celebrate her death. Mary, who would later be nicknamed "Bloody Mary", attempted to return England to Catholicism at any cost. This, coupled with her links to Spain, ensured that much of her reign was unsuccessful.

THE CORONATION OF ENGLAND'S FIRST RULING QUEEN

Mary was the first woman to be crowned as Queen of England in her own right. She was determined that the ceremony should be magnificent. On 28 September 1553, she sailed to the Tower of London, accompanied by much of the nobility. The route of the river procession was lined with boats all decked out with streamers and carrying the mayor and aldermen of the city. When the queen arrived at the Tower, guns were fired in celebration.

The next day was spent at the Tower where Mary appointed 15 new Knights of the Bath. On 30 September, she processed through the streets of London, showing herself to the people. She rode in a rich chariot drawn by six horses. For the journey, Mary wore a dress of blue velvet, trimmed with ermine and, on her head, sat a gold circlet that was so heavy that she was forced to hold up her head with her hands. Much of the nobility rode with her, including her half-sister, Princess Elizabeth, and former stepmother, Anne of Cleves, who shared the second coach. Anne was, by that time, the last survivor of the six wives of Henry VIII and would live for another four years.

The following day, Mary walked in procession to Westminster Abbey where she was crowned as Queen of England. Her mother had raised her as a potential future queen and the new monarch was triumphant. She was acutely aware, however, that as an unmarried female ruler she was an oddity and that she was expected to marry and provide England with a king.

MARY'S APPEARANCE

Mary Tudor had been a golden-haired, pretty and promising child who was much admired at her father's court. By the time she came to the throne in 1553, however, she was in her late 30s and ageing. She had always been small and had a surprisingly deep voice which sounded mannish to her contemporaries. She loved fine clothes and jewels but dressed badly with no flair for fashion.

Mary's life was blighted by her parents' divorce and one of her first acts as queen was to repeal the divorce and declare herself legitimate once more. This gave her a great deal of personal satisfaction although the new queen, who loved children, longed for marriage and an heir. She was a kind woman, taking an interest in her little half-sister, Elizabeth, after the child's mother was executed. She also enjoyed spending time with her cousins and friends. She had received no training after her parents' divorce in how to be a monarch.

WYATT'S REBELLION

No one expected a woman to rule alone and speculation was rife about who Mary would marry. In November 1553 she received a proposal from Prince Philip of Spain (1527–1598), which she readily accepted.

The announcement of Mary's marriage was not greeted favourably by everyone in England. Her leading councillor, Stephen Gardiner, Bishop of Winchester (1497–1555), considered that "it would be difficult to induce the people to consent to a foreigner". The bishop instead pushed for a marriage to his friend, Edward Courtenay (1526–1556), who was a descendant of Edward IV.

The announcement of the Spanish marriage caused mutterings of discontent throughout England and, by the end of 1553, a conspiracy had been formed aiming to depose Mary and place her half-sister – who would be married to Courtenay – on the throne. It was intended that there would be four strands to the rebellion. A rising in Herefordshire would be led by Sir James Croft (1518–1590), one in the south-west by Sir Peter Carew (c.1514–1575) and Edward Courtenay (c.1527–1556) and a rebellion in Leicestershire by the Duke of Suffolk, the father of the imprisoned Lady Jane Grey (1517–1554). The fourth uprising, in Kent, was to be led by Sir Thomas Wyatt the Younger (1521–1554).

Courtenay proved to be the conspiracy's downfall. Thanks to his royal blood, the young man had spent half his life in the Tower. As such, he was politically naive and, on 21 January 1554, confessed everything to Stephen Gardiner. The bishop immediately informed Mary.

On 25 January 1554, only four days after Courtenay's confession, Sir Thomas Wyatt rode into the marketplace at Maidstone in Kent and issued a proclamation setting out his justification for rebellion. He saw his rebellion as a "quarrel against the Strangers", whom he feared would overrun England following the queen's Spanish marriage. The English had always been suspicious of foreigners and Wyatt's words were well received. As people flocked to him, he made his way to Rochester. Forewarned, Mary sent out a royal army as Wyatt moved on to Dartford, where he spent the night of 31 January. All attempts to either negotiate or engage with the rebels came to nothing.

As Wyatt's force moved towards London, Mary took decisive action, going herself to the Guildhall in London to speak to the people. To the assembled crowd, the queen claimed that her marriage had only been arranged with the consent and advice of her council, before declaring that it could only ever be her second marriage, since "I am already married to the Common Weal and the faithful members of the same; the spousal ring whereof I have on my finger: which never hitherto was, nor hereafter shall be, left off". As a woman married to her people, there was nothing "more acceptable to my heart, nor more answerable to my will, than your advancement in wealth and welfare, with the furtherance of God's glory".

The speech saved the situation. On 3 February Wyatt reached Southwark, where he found London Bridge defended and the gates locked. In the 16th century there were only a few ways to cross the Thames without using a ferry and this was a major setback to Wyatt. On 6 February, after reconsidering his tactics, he set out westward to Kingston Bridge and crossed without incident. By the next morning, he had reached Hyde Park, causing a general panic in London and at court. Mary, who was at Whitehall, was urged to flee with the cry of "All is lost! Away! Away! A Barge! A Barge!" Once again, she took control, telling those around her that they should "fall to prayer! And I warrant you, we shall hear better news anon". She declared confidently that God "in whom my chief trust is" would not deceive her.

Although in command of a large army, Wyatt's troops were unruly. When faced with royal forces, he failed to maintain control and was quickly captured and taken to the Tower. For Mary, who viewed her accession as miraculous, this was further proof of God's favour. None of the other strands of the rebellion came to much, although the Duke of Suffolk, who had ridden northwards, was found hiding in a hollow tree and returned as a prisoner to London. Suffolk's conduct signed Lady Jane Grey's death warrant and father and daughter were executed soon afterwards. Wyatt was also beheaded, while Princess Elizabeth, whom he had implicated, was imprisoned in the Tower.

PRINCESS ELIZABETH IN THE TOWER

On 17 March 1554, two days after Wyatt's trial, Princess Elizabeth was informed that a barge was waiting to take her, as a prisoner, to the Tower of London. Alarmed, she asked for leave to send a letter to the queen. Elizabeth sat down to write, begging that she "be not condemned without answer and proof", before declaring that "I protest before God I never practised, counselled or consented to anything prejudicial to you or dangerous to the state". She begged for a personal interview "before I go to the Tower (if possible)". Mary had no intention of seeing her half-sister, but the delay in writing the "tide letter" meant that the tide had changed, giving the princess one further precious night of freedom before she was moved to the ancient fortress the next day.

Elizabeth's own mother had never emerged from the Tower following her arrest in May 1536 and the princess was understandably terrified. As she stepped out of the boat, she cried out "Oh Lord! I never thought to have come in here as prisoner; and I pray you all good friends and fellows, bear me witness, that I come in no traitor, but as true a woman to the queen's majesty as any is now living; and thereon will I take my death". Elizabeth knew that she had been implicated in the rebellion by Wyatt, who claimed to have written to her, and she was frightened. Glancing round, she noticed the armed men standing close at hand and asked "What! Are all these harnessed men here for me?" When this was denied, she answered "I know it is so; it needed not for me, being, alas! but a weak woman".

When Elizabeth finally entered, two of the assembled peers began to lock the doors of her prison before the Earl of Sussex cautioned them to take care, since "she was a king's daughter, and is the queen's sister". Aware that Elizabeth was, potentially, their future mistress he urged them to "go no further than your commission".

Elizabeth spent a nervous two months in the Tower before finally moving to house arrest at the rundown manor of Woodstock. Although still a prisoner, the danger had passed and, with crowds lining the road to her place of exile, she appeared to be making a triumphal progress. The princess spent nearly a year there before finally being allowed to return to court to act as one of the witnesses to the birth of a child that the queen hoped would supplant her.

THE SPANISH MARRIAGE

Mary had always relied on the advice of her cousin, the Holy Roman Emperor, Charles V. Soon after her accession she informed the Imperial Ambassador, Simon Renard, that she would be guided by Charles in her choice of a husband. As the most eligible woman in Europe, Mary was bombarded with suitors but the only husband she really wanted was Philip of Spain – a 26-year-old widower and the eldest son of her beloved cousin. Philip was a serious-minded and religious young man and was prepared to marry his older kinswoman, proposing to her in November 1553. Mary at first, coyly, protested that she was too old for Philip, before joyously accepting.

The prince landed at Southampton on 19 July 1554 and moved on to Winchester where the couple met. One of his attendants complained that Mary looked older than they had expected and dressed badly. Philip for his part hid any disappointment, while his bride immediately fell in love with him. The queen was a romantic and, although they had a grand marriage in Winchester Cathedral on 25 July 1554, she asked touchingly for a plain gold hoop for her wedding ring "because maidens were so married in old times". At her request, her husband was declared King of England during her lifetime. In order to ensure that there was no disparity in rank between the couple, Charles resigned the kingdoms of Naples and Sicily to his son before the ceremony.

TWO PHANTOM PREGNANCIES

At the time of her marriage, Mary was 38-years-old and well past the usual age for childbearing in that period. Her mother had failed to become pregnant after the age of 33 and there were considerable doubts that she would be able to safeguard the succession with the birth of her own child.

Mary had no such worries, believing that God would provide her with an heir. She was thrilled in September 1554 to be told by her physicians that she was expecting a child and, as the months passed, she showed all the signs of pregnancy. At Easter 1555 the queen went into confinement at Hampton Court to await the birth of her child. It was believed that the baby was due in May and the queen, as a first-time mother, ensured that everything was ready for the baby's arrival – with midwifes, rockers and nurses employed, as well as a cradle prepared.

Shortly after Mary went into confinement, word that she had given birth to a healthy son passed through London, with bells rung, bonfires lit and ceremonial processions of thanksgiving made. The news spread to Antwerp, which was ruled by Philip's aunt, Mary of Hungary, who paid rewards to those that brought her the news. Word even reached the baby's grandfather, Charles V, before it was revealed that it was only a rumour and that the queen continued to wait at Hampton Court.

Mary was still confident that there would be a child but, as May passed, her physicians began to recalculate, saying first that there would be a birth in June and then July. As time wore on, the people around the queen became increasingly sceptical while there were rumours that she had sent agents into London in an attempt to buy a male child to pass off as her own. Mary, however, continued to wait but, as her swollen stomach began to reduce in size, even she was forced to admit the truth. Early in August, the court abruptly left Hampton Court – a tacit acknowledgement that there would be no baby. Mary, who was desperate for a child, had suffered a phantom pregnancy. On 29 August 1555, Philip left England for Flanders.

Mary did not see her husband again until March 1557 when Philip, who had become King of Spain, landed at Dover in an attempt to persuade his wife to join him in a war against France. Mary was overjoyed to see him, but the visit lasted only four months and would be his last. Once again, she believed that she had conceived a child, but her claims were greeted with a good degree of scepticism. So certain was she, however, that she made a will in March 1558 bequeathing the crown to her child. Once again, there was no baby, although on this occasion the queen at least had the good sense not to make a public show of entering confinement.

Her failure to provide England with a Catholic heir led Mary to believe that she had incurred God's displeasure in some way. As a result she increased her efforts to return England to Catholicism.

BURNING HERETICS

Mary's poor reputation rests largely on the burnings that she carried out in an attempt to rid England of Protestantism.

The queen passionately believed in her Roman Catholic faith and had a genuine desire to save the souls of her subjects and return England to its loyalty to the pope. She faced her first religious dilemma upon coming to the throne with the funeral of her Protestant half-brother, Edward VI. Mary announced that she would hold a Catholic funeral for him, something which horrified even the Imperial Ambassador, Simon Renard, who was concerned that the Londoners would rise up against her for going against her brother's wishes. Instead, the queen compromised, allowing Edward to be buried in accordance with his

Protestant faith, while holding a private Requiem Mass for his soul. Even this caused a backlash, with a Catholic priest attacked by a mob in the pulpit at St Paul's on the Sunday after the funeral.

Mary was not usually prepared to make any compromises for her faith. Before the end of July 1553, she had written to ask the pope to return England to his authority. She also ordered mass to be performed openly at court and in London. Pressure was put on Princess Elizabeth to attend, and it did not help relations between them when she spent much of her first service loudly complaining that her stomach hurt.

As part of her attempt to rid England of Protestantism, Mary began to burn "heretics" in early 1555. Many ordinary people suffered during her reign, as well as more high-profile victims, such as Thomas Cranmer, Archbishop of Canterbury.

Mary had a personal grudge against Cranmer, the man who had pronounced the annulment of her parents' marriage. The queen had been further angered by his role in Lady Jane Grey's usurpation of the throne, and she had no intention of pardoning him when he was accused of heresy. In an attempt to save his life and after considerable pressure was placed on him, Cranmer recanted his Protestant faith and recognized the pope as head of the church, but it was not enough. He went to the stake at Oxford on 21 March 1556, declaring that his recantation was insincere while on the scaffold. He thrust his right hand first into the flames, since it was that hand which had signed his recantation.

Mary was not the only Tudor monarch to burn heretics, but the number killed in only four years, was startling.

Mary fell ill in May 1558, with the Spanish ambassador reporting that she was both weak and depressed from the failure of her second "pregnancy". Her health did not improve and, by November, she was seriously unwell. There was an outbreak of influenza in late 1558, which would carry off Mary's Archbishop of Canterbury. This also hastened the queen's own death and, by the first week of November, it was clear that she was dying. Her reputation was so poor that her death on 17 November 1558 went largely unlamented, with people instead flocking to the new queen, Elizabeth I, at Hatfield.

10

THE VIRGIN QUEEN

Born 7 September 1533
Died 24 March 1603
Reigned 17 November 1558–25 March 1603

The last Tudor monarch, Elizabeth I, had the most improbable path to the throne. Born the daughter of Henry VIII and Anne Boleyn in 1533, she was declared illegitimate after her mother's execution. Elizabeth finally returned to court in the 1540s when she was reinstated in the succession along with her elder half-sister, Mary. With only one son, Henry VIII had considered the succession to be vulnerable. He therefore added both his daughters as heirs in the third Act of Succession of 1543, although, since they remained legally illegitimate, any younger children born to Henry's sixth wife, Catherine Parr, would have preceded them. Her unlikely road to the throne was also a dangerous one with half-siblings Edward VI disinheriting her in favour of Lady Jane Grey and Mary imprisoning her. Following the failure of Mary's "pregnancy" in 1555, Elizabeth's succession had, however, become only a matter of time.

THE COUNT OF FERIA'S VISIT

In November 1558, Elizabeth received a visit from the Spanish Count of Feria at her house at Hatfield in Hertfordshire. Feria had arrived in England that month to find Queen Mary dying and her councillors in a state of terror about what the next monarch planned to do with them. Feria, who was the ambassador of Mary's husband, King Philip II of Spain, was anxious to ensure continuing friendly relations with England. He set out to visit Elizabeth to assure her of Philip's support.

Elizabeth was happy to speak with Feria, but the ambassador did not find her as malleable as he had hoped. Instead, the Spaniard was confronted with "a very vain and clever woman", who had "been thoroughly schooled in the manner in which her father conducted his affairs". He had grave doubts about the princess's religious affiliations since, although she attended mass during her sister's reign, it was well known that her household was staffed by Protestant sympathizers.

Elizabeth was also still highly indignant about the way that she had been treated during her sister's reign. When Feria suggested that it was Philip who had helped smooth the way for her to take the throne she stopped him, declaring that "it was the people who put her in her present position and she will not acknowledge that Your Majesty or the nobility of this realm had any part in it". Feria left the interview certain that Elizabeth meant to be ruled by no one, least of all her Spanish brother-in-law.

In this, he was to be proved right. On the morning of 17 November 1558, Sir Nicholas Throckmorton (c.1515–1571) set out from London for Hatfield, bearing Mary's betrothal ring as proof of her death. He was overtaken on the road by two members of the former queen's council: the Earls of Arundel and Pembroke. Upon their arrival at Hatfield, the pair found Elizabeth sitting under an oak tree, some distance from the house. She was reading the New Testament in Greek but looked up when they arrived.

Upon being informed that she was now queen, Elizabeth was overcome with emotion, unable to speak for a few moments before she composed herself and praised God. The new Queen of England was jubilant, declaring that "it is the Lord's doing and it is marvellous in our eyes".

ELIZABETH'S APPEARANCE

Elizabeth was 25-years-old and in her youthful prime at the time of her accession. While never a beauty, she was attractive enough and the historian John Hawyward (c.1564–1627) described her as being "of stature mean, slender, straight and amiably composed; of such state in her carriage, as every motion of her seemed to bear majesty". She had fair hair "inclined to pale yellow", with "lively and sweet" eyes and a nose that rose slightly in the middle.

Portraits suggest that Elizabeth resembled her mother facially, although she had her father's colouring. During her brother's reign, she had sought to present herself as a modest Protestant maiden, refusing to wear the rich clothes and jewels that had been left to her by her father. Throughout this time, she was held up as a model to other young women, making them "ashamed to be dressed and painted like peacocks" as John Aylmer (1521–1594), Bishop and tutor to Lady Jane Grey, put it. Even the sober Lady Jane Grey herself declared that, in matters of dress, she wished to follow "my Lady Elizabeth which followeth God's word". Elizabeth began to dress more flamboyantly during her sister's reign and it is clear that sombre black was not her real preference.

As queen, Elizabeth loved fine clothes and was proud of her appearance, growing concerned as she began to notice herself ageing. From her 40s and 50s she wore wigs to cover her grey hair and thick layers of make-up to give the illusion of eternal youth. Her clothes also grew increasingly elaborate with large ruffs and huge padded sleeves; she owned around 3,000 costly gowns, many of which were strewn with jewels. She continued to attract suitors into her old age, with young men, such as Walter Raleigh (c.1552–1618) and the Earl of Essex, encouraging her in the belief that time had stood still for her.

The personal possessions with which she decorated her palaces were equally splendid. She carried golden clocks around with her from residence to residence, as well as books covered in silver gilt and a bed pane embroidered with silver fabric. An inventory of the her possessions noted that she also owned more exotic items, including a "staff of unicorn's horn with a cross garnished with silver gilt". It was topped with a crystal ball.

ELIZABETH'S COUNCIL

While she was still at Hatfield, Elizabeth began assembling her council. William Cecil, who had served both Edward and Mary was particularly favoured as her Principal Secretary of State, while Robert Dudley (1532–1588) – the son of the executed Duke of Northumberland – became her master of horse.

As a hint of the nature of the new regime, Elizabeth retained only 10 of her sister's 44 councillors. There was a place for her relatives, including her great-uncle, Lord William Howard (c.1510–1573) and Sir Francis Knollys (c.1511–1596), who had married her cousin. It also had a distinctly Protestant flavour. Knollys had actually left England during Mary's reign to avoid living under a Catholic regime, while her step-uncle, William Parr, Marquis of Northampton (1513–1571) was a fervent Protestant.

From 1558, the council tended to meet three times a week, although this increased in frequency later in the reign.

WILLIAM CECIL (1520–1598)

William Cecil was appointed to head Elizabeth's Privy Council on her accession and she relied on his advice until his death. He had been born in 1520 and educated first at grammar school and then Cambridge, before undertaking training in the law. His father had served at court and Cecil was able to use his abilities and court connections to secure the position of private secretary to Protector Somerset in 1548. He shared his patron's Protestant faith, but served under Mary.

He was well known to Elizabeth as the surveyor of her lands and the pair were in contact during the last days of the Marian government. In 1558, the new queen trusted him, informing him at his appointment "This judgment I have of you, that you will not be corrupted by any manner of gift, and that you will be faithful to the state, and that without respect of my private will, you will give me that counsel you think best".

Cecil worked hard for Elizabeth. Although the pair sometimes quarrelled and often disagreed, the queen relied on her secretary's good judgment. Cecil, who was created Lord Burghley by his mistress, groomed his son, Robert, to succeed him. He was still active until a few weeks before his death, finally retiring ill to his bed in July 1598. The queen visited and fed soup to him herself, but, for the 78-year-old, the end had come. He died on 4 August 1598.

ELIZABETH'S CORONATION

Elizabeth was highly popular with the people of England, showing herself to them regularly and interacting with the crowds around her. On 14 January 1559, the new queen left the Tower of London to process through the city on the day before her coronation. As usual, she was greeted with crowds wishing her well, to which she gave "Hearty thanks!" When people cried out "God save her Grace!", she replied "God save them all!", winning further approval from the crowd.

The route of Elizabeth's progress was lined with pageants, which she watched from her chariot, with a canopy over her head. She pleased her subjects by stopping to take flowers offered to her, as well as speaking to those that performed before her. She spent that night at Westminster Palace. The following day, she was crowned queen by the Bishop of Carlisle.

TUDOR WOMEN

Until the accession of Mary I, the idea of being ruled by a woman was an alien one in England. Even with a ruling queen, women remained second-class citizens in Elizabethan England. Married women could hold no property. Unmarried women of any age who had inherited land were held in wardship by the crown. This meant that they were unable to marry without royal consent, on pain of forfeiting their lands.

Much higher standards of behaviour were expected of women than men. Unlike their husbands, women were required to be faithful, as well as submissive to men. Home was their domain and, while educating women had become fashionable earlier in the Tudor period, most lower-status girls received little, if any, tuition. Girls of all classes were raised for marriage, with upper-class girls taught music and needlework and lower-class girls given a grounding in the skills required to run a house. Ensuring that a girl remained a virgin was of paramount importance to her mother. Juan Luis Vives (1493–1540) in *The Education of a Christian Woman* even argued that dancing, with its "shaking and bragging and uncleanly handlings gropings and kissings" was "a very kindling of lechery". Ideally, the writer felt, daughters should remain inside the house as much as possible.

For lower-status women, it was not possible to remain in the home. Although women were forbidden from attending university and could not enter a profession, such as that of lawyer or doctor, they could take paid work. Women could be apprenticed in a craft and join a guild, although most working women in Tudor

England took on unskilled labour. Roles open to women included washerwoman, servant, brewer or weaver. In spite of their low status, they made up a sizeable portion of the workforce.

LADY CATHERINE GREY (1540–1568)

As soon as Mary I's death was announced the 16-year-old Mary, Queen of Scots, who was living in France, proclaimed herself Queen of England. There was some justification for this claim, since the marriage of Elizabeth's parents was of doubtful validity and she was legally illegitimate. The young Scottish queen was the only child of James V of Scotland, who was the only son of Henry VIII's eldest sister. She therefore had an excellent claim to the throne. Very few people in England were, however, prepared to abandon the English and popular Elizabeth in favour of a Catholic foreigner.

Mary was not necessarily even Elizabeth's heir. Under the terms of Henry VIII's will, in which he disregarded the descendants of his elder sister, Elizabeth was the true queen, with his niece, Frances Brandon (1517–1559), and her surviving daughters, Catherine (1540–1568) and Mary Grey (1545–1578), the next heirs. Since Frances Brandon had previously agreed to be passed over in favour of her eldest daughter, the unfortunate Lady Jane Grey, many considered her second daughter, Catherine, to be heir to the throne.

Being heir to the throne was dangerous, particularly since Elizabeth heartily disliked her Grey cousins. The peril was brought home to Catherine in the summer of 1559 on the discovery of a plot to kidnap her. The conspirators intended to bring her to Spain, where she would be married either to the son of King Philip "or some other of lesser degree". A second plot the following year intended that Catherine would be stolen away to Scotland to marry the Earl of Arran. The international interest in her cousin worried Elizabeth, who brought the girl into her privy chamber in order to keep her under close watch. At the same time she insincerely declared that she considered Catherine to be her daughter and that she wanted to formally adopt her.

Although Catherine Grey came to court in 1560, she was not as closely watched as she should have been. While at court she fell in love with Edward Seymour (1539–1621), Earl of Hertford, who had once been betrothed to her sister, Jane. Both of the young couples' mothers gave their consent to the match. The pair neglected, however, to obtain the queen's approval, marrying in secret in December 1560. Unfortunately, neither Hertford nor Catherine caught the name of the auburn-bearded priest who officiated, while the only other witness, Hertford's consumptive sister, died on 20 March 1561. This proved to be calamitous when, at the end of July 1561, the heavily pregnant Catherine finally confessed. As far as Elizabeth was concerned, with no witnesses, there had been no wedding and the couple were sent to the Tower. When Catherine bore a son in September, he was declared illegitimate, remaining in the Tower with his imprisoned parents.

Catherine's moment nearly came in 1562. The queen, who was then at Hampton Court, suddenly felt unwell on 10 October and decided to have a bath. It was soon realized that she was suffering from the deadly smallpox. Bishop Álvaro de la Quadra (?–1564), Spanish Ambassador to England noted that "the cold caught by leaving her bath for the air resulted in so violent a fever" that, after seven days of illness, she was considered to be on the point of death.

Smallpox, which, caused eruptions on the face and body of a sufferer was highly dangerous, with the queen "all but gone", according to Bishop de la Quadra. On 16 October Elizabeth's council met to discuss the succession, but were much divided. Most wanted Catherine Grey, who was still in the Tower. Others, who Bishop de la Quadra said "found flaw" in Henry VIII's will, elected the Plantagenet Earl of Huntingdon (1535–1595). The earl, who was only in his mid-20s, owed his royal blood to his mother's grandmother, Margaret Pole, Countess of Salisbury, who was Edward IV's niece, as well as to his father, who was descended from Edward III. The earl died before Elizabeth, in 1595, and never pressed his claims. However, the fact that he was both a man and Protestant meant that he was always a popular choice.

In 1562 Lady Catherine Grey was potentially only one fading heartbeat from the throne but, to the surprise of everyone, the queen rallied, in spite of the fact that, as she later admitted, "death possessed almost every joint of me". Catherine remained a prisoner for the rest of her life, causing further scandal when brief meetings with her imprisoned husband in the Tower resulted in the birth of a second son on 10 February 1563. After the birth she was kept apart from her husband until her early death on 27 January 1568.

With Catherine Grey's sons' illegitimacy, her sister Mary became heir to the throne, unless, of course, the queen married and produced an heir of her own.

11

MARRIED TO MY COUNTRY

Elizabeth was unmarried when she came to the throne. It was unheard of for a female sovereign to rule alone and everyone expected that she would soon marry in order to give England a king. At the same time, as the last of Henry VIII's children, she needed to produce an heir if the Tudor dynasty was to endure. She received marriage proposals until well into her 50s, but always refused them. In a speech to her first Parliament in February 1559 she ended by declaring that "lastly, this may be sufficient, both for my memory and honour of my name, if when I have expired my last breath, this may be inscribed upon my tomb: here lies interred Elizabeth, A virgin pure until her death".

PHILIP OF SPAIN (1527–1598)

Elizabeth had attracted suitors even before she came to the throne, turning down the Prince of Sweden early in 1558 by claiming that she wished to remain a virgin. Such offers intensified when she became queen. In January 1559 even her brother-in-law, Philip of Spain, offered himself unwillingly, believing that marriage to Elizabeth was the best way to ensure that England remained Catholic. The queen, who was as unenthusiastic about marriage to Philip as he was about her, kept negotiations open until March 1559, when she had agreed peace with France and no longer needed peace with Spain.

In spite of the loss of England, Philip was personally relieved not to retain a personal involvement in the country. His cousin, the Ferdinand II, Archduke of Austria (1529–1595), soon presented himself as a suitor to Elizabeth. When this match also came to nothing, Ferdinand's younger brother proposed. Archduke Charles (1540–1590), as a younger son, was considerably more persistent than his brother and the queen managed to drag the courtship out for seven years.

Elizabeth always insisted that her suitors visit her in England, arguing that she could not marry a man that she had never seen. This brought negotiations to a standstill since a man as important as the Archduke Charles could not be expected to come without a promise of marriage. Not all princes heeded this, however, and Elizabeth was considerably alarmed when John of Finland, the younger son of the King of Sweden, arrived unexpectedly to woo her in October 1559.

Elizabeth declared that she was insulted when the Archduke Charles finally married another woman, but she had never seriously considered him. For the Virgin Queen, marriage negotiations were an excellent way of ensuring friendly relationships with foreign powers. There was, however, one foreign prince that she did come close to marrying.

 FRANCIS, DUKE OF ALENCON (1555–1584)

Early in 1565 the 14-year-old Charles IX (1550–1574) of France proposed marriage to Elizabeth although, for the 31-year-old queen, this was never an attractive proposition. Charles also had two younger brothers for whom their mother, Catherine de Medici (1519–1589), was anxious to provide. Henry, Duke of Anjou (1551–1589), who would later be King of France, reluctantly offered himself in 1571. However, once again, the age gap proved difficult, particularly when the duke disparagingly referred to her as an old woman with a sore leg. A still-younger brother, Francis, Duke of Alencon (1555–1584), was suggested instead, but this also came to nothing at the time.

Unlike his older brothers, Alencon (who became Duke of Anjou when his brother succeeded as Henry III) had no kingdom to inherit. He was therefore very interested in marriage to Elizabeth, with negotiations opening once again in the spring of 1578. He was then aged 23 and more than two decades younger than the woman whom he professed to adore. He was eager to win a kingdom, however, and sent his friend, Jean de Simier, to England to suggest the marriage.

Elizabeth always had an eye for a handsome man and was very taken with the charming de Simier, nicknaming him her monkey. Unlike so many foreign princes before him, Alencon was prepared to personally court the queen, arriving in August 1578. Elizabeth had heard rumours that the French prince was very short and disfigured by smallpox, yet she was pleased with what she saw, finding him attractive and dashing. He was also granted a playful nickname: her frog, and the pair were inseparable for two weeks. She would later write to him, confirming that "For my part, I confess that there is no prince in the world to whom I would more willingly yield to be his, than to yourself, nor to whom I think myself more obliged, nor with whom I would pass the years of my life".

The queen was emotional on Alencon's departure, finding herself torn between her heart and her head. Her physicians assured her that she could still bear a child although, at 45, she must have had doubts. Similarly, a marriage with a French Catholic would never be popular in England.

As a mark of her turmoil, Elizabeth composed a poem on Alencon's return to France, declaring that:

> I grieve and are not show my discontent;
> I love, and yet am forced to seem to hate;
> I do, yet dare not say I ever meant;
> I seem stark mute, but inwardly do prate
> I am, and not; I freeze and yet am burned,
> Since from myself another self I turned.

Alencon proved to be a lasting suitor and, during a visit in November 1581, she finally bowed to her heart and agreed to marry him – the only marriage proposal she would ever accept. That night, while listening to her maids talking about the dangers of childbirth, she changed her mind.

The following day she informed Alencon personally that, while they would remain betrothed, they could never marry. Disgruntled, the prince refused to go, finally being bribed away in February 1582 with £60,000 and three English warships to assist in his campaigns in the Netherlands. The queen kept up the pretence of her betrothal to Alencon, ordering her court into mourning when he died in 1584. She also sent her condolences to his mother, declaring that "For inasmuch as you are his mother, so it is that there remain to you several other children. But for me, I find no consolation except death, which I hope will soon reunite us. Madame, if you were able to see the image of my heart, you would see the portrait of a body without a soul". He was the man that she came closest to marrying and also her last serious suitor.

THE NATIONAL LOTTERY

Elizabeth's reign saw the creation of the National Lottery in 1567. This lottery, which was held with the purpose of raising funds for ship building, had a prize of £5,000, with tickets on sale at ten shillings each. The ticket price, which was approximately half of a labourer's weekly wage, would have placed it beyond the reach of most people, although there was an added incentive offered. Anyone who took part was granted immunity from prosecution from all but the most serious crimes.

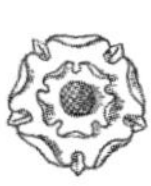

THE DEATH OF AMY ROBSART (1532–1560)

Elizabeth did not have only foreign suitors. She also had a number of English favourites, some of whom hoped to marry her. The most prominent was Robert Dudley (1532–1588), the son of the executed Duke of Northumberland and a man who was almost exactly the same age as the queen. The pair had been prisoners in the Tower at the same time during Mary's reign and this forged a bond between them. Dudley was handsome and charismatic and Elizabeth was utterly charmed by him, making him her master of horse and a knight of the garter at her accession. Elizabeth's preference for Dudley mystified her contemporaries, with one commenting that he appeared to have few virtues, unless he gave what the historian William Camden (1551–1623) described as "some shadowed tokens" that only the queen could see.

By early 1559 it was whispered that Elizabeth and Dudley were lovers and that they intended to marry as soon as his wife, Amy Robsart, was dead. The pair did little to scotch the rumours, appearing to be in love at court. He went so far as to ask for Spanish assistance in persuading the queen to marry him. The Spanish ambassador, for one, certainly believed that he was a strong contender for Elizabeth's hand, writing to his master that there were rumours that the queen had been seen visiting Dudley in his chamber both during the day and at night.

Elizabeth was well aware of Amy Robsart's existence, but chose to ignore her, making it plain that she did not want her to come to court. Instead Amy spent her time in the countryside and, in September 1560, was staying with friends in Abingdon. On the morning of 8 September 1560, Dudley's wife, who was in poor health, insisted that her servants visit a local fair, something which meant that only she and two other women remained in the house. That evening, when the servants returned, they found Amy lying dead at the bottom of a flight of steps with a broken neck.

When news of the death reached Elizabeth she was shocked into speechlessness. The queen realized at once just how terrible the death of her rival looked, and ordered Dudley to leave court while it was investigated.

Unsurprisingly, the inquiry returned a verdict of accidental death, holding that Amy had fallen down the stairs. This is possible although, given her strange behaviour in emptying the house, as well as the evidence of some of her ladies, suicide would seem a strong possibility. Most people simply believed that Dudley had murdered his wife. The suspicion remained with him for the rest of his life, making it impossible for the queen to ever consider marrying the man she loved.

Dudley continued to hope for some years but, in 1578, he secretly married the queen's cousin, Lettice Knollys, whom he had met at court. He hoped to keep the marriage private but, when Jean de Simier heard of it in the middle of 1578, he informed the queen personally, hoping that it would turn Elizabeth more firmly towards his master, Francis, Duke of Alencon.

Elizabeth was devastated when she heard the news, banning Lettice from court. Although she would later reconcile with Dudley, she always refused to see his wife, forcing her to remain in exile for the remainder of the reign.

BOTTLED BEER

As Elizabeth involved herself in marriage negotiations, one of her subjects made an innovative discovery. In 1568, the dean of St Paul's poured some beer into a bottle in order to take it on a fishing trip. He mislaid his drink but, when he discovered it some days later, found that it was still drinkable. The idea of storing beer in bottles had not been considered before, with the Dean finding himself an accidental inventor. Beer and ale were very widely drunk in Tudor times. Before Catherine of Aragon arrived in England to marry Prince Arthur, she had been advised by her mother to practise drinking ale to ensure that she built up a tolerance and did not spend her first weeks in her new homeland tipsy. English water was widely considered to be undrinkable and everyone, including children, drank ale.

LADY MARY GREY (1545–1578)

While Elizabeth was averse to the idea of marriage, her Grey cousins were eager to take husbands and start their own families. Red-haired and freckled, Mary Grey was less than four feet tall and was never an entirely credible candidate for the throne in contemporaries' eyes.

Elizabeth disliked Mary as much as she hated Catherine and had no plans to arrange a marriage for her. Like her sister, Mary took matters into her own hands, secretly marrying Thomas (or, in some sources, Martin) Keyes (1524–1571), the low-born sergeant-porter at Westminster Palace, whom she had met while she was staying with the court.

Quite apart from the difference in the couple's status, Keyes was a striking choice for the diminutive Mary. He was a giant of a man, standing at six feet eight inches tall. He was also twice her age and a widower with at least six children. Keyes at least showed the lonely Mary some attention, making her several gifts during their courtship.

Mary and Keyes married secretly on 10 August 1565 at Westminster Palace. Aware of the challenge to her sister's marriage, Mary took the precaution of ensuring that, as well as the priest, Keyes' brother, one of his friends and two servants were present to witness the ceremony.

Word of the marriage reached the queen within two weeks and, furious, she committed them both to prison. The couple were never able to live together, with Keyes dying in September 1571. Mary, who took his death "grievously" according to Lord Cobham, was finally released from captivity in 1573. The woman who was legally heir to Elizabeth's throne died on 20 April 1578, leaving the English succession once again unresolved.

12

THE HERETIC QUEEN

Although she had conformed to Catholicism, Elizabeth was well known to have Protestant sympathies. Unlike her brother, who had been a fervent Protestant, she was content to tread a middle way. It was once said of the queen that she did not wish to make windows into men's souls, something which characterized her religious policies. What she required of her subjects was obedience in matters of religion, not necessarily also conformity of belief. The punishments for disobedience could, however, be oppressive.

A RELIGIOUS SETTLEMENT

Elizabeth allowed a requiem mass to be celebrated during Mary I's funeral. She had attended mass during her sister's reign, but few were under any illusion that she meant to keep England Catholic. As a result, she struggled to find a bishop to officiate at her coronation. Mary's Archbishop of Canterbury, Cardinal Pole, had recently died, while the Archbishop of York and all but the Bishop of Carlisle refused to act. The first sign of religious change came at Christmas 1558 when Elizabeth left mass before communion was given. She also issued a proclamation on 28 December declaring that parts of the services in parish churches were once again to be conducted in English.

The Act of Supremacy was passed in 1559, which confirmed the changes to the state's religion and Elizabeth's governorship of the Church of England. The Act of Uniformity, which was passed at the same time, ordered that an amended version of Edward VI's 1552 prayer book should be used in all churches.

Elizabeth considered herself to be Head of the Church of England, although she accepted the title of Supreme Governor when concerns were raised about a woman taking the headship. Although sincere in her beliefs, she was no extremist and attempted to tread a middle path, between the staunch Protestantism of her brother's reign and Mary's Catholicism. One of her first acts was to name her mother's former chaplain, Matthew Parker (1540–1590), as Archbishop of Canterbury, a man that she had known all her life. She also appointed a number of other Protestants. In spite of her moderate course she was certainly a Protestant and, as the reign progressed, Catholicism came to be almost synonymous with disloyalty and treason.

CHURCH PAPISTS

At Elizabeth's accession, many people in England held trad-itional Catholic religious beliefs. England's religion had changed dramatically and rapidly over the previous few decades and, in 1559, few believed that the Act of Supremacy would be the final word.

At first, the penalties for recusancy – the failure to attend Protestant church services – were not that great. Non-attendance was always punishable by fines but, in 1587, these were increased to the vast sum of £260 per year per person. In the event that a person could not pay (and most could not), the crown seized two-thirds of their property. Recusants were also vulnerable to imprisonment, with some Catholics spending decades locked away.

As a result of this, recusancy was only chosen by the most committed Catholics, while the vast majority instead attended church services. These church Papists employed a number of strategies to ensure that they were not seen to be active participants, for example, praying in Latin while the service went on or standing too far from the priest to hear the Protestant service. Sometimes families chose one member to be a recusant and pay the fines. For example, a gentleman named Thomas Blount, of Astley in Shropshire, attended church during the lifetime of his wife, Frances, who was a recusant. After her death, he became a recusant himself until the fines became too much to bear.

PRIEST HOLES

Elizabethan houses can still surprise their owners more than 400 years after they were built. Mapledurham House in Oxfordshire, for example, which was owned by Elizabeth's lieutenant of the Tower, revealed a priest hole underneath a sliding hearth as recently as 2002.

Being a Catholic priest in Elizabethan England was highly dangerous and many were executed or imprisoned. Priest holes were secret spaces, chambers or passageways concealed within large houses. They were designed to function as a hiding place for a Catholic priest resident in the house. In the 1590s, Scotney Castle in Sussex was searched twice by local officials, who believed that Catholic priests were harboured there.

During the first search, a Jesuit, Father Richard Blount (1565–1638), was hiding in a priest hole below the stairs with one servant. They had few provisions and, when these had been exhausted, Blount's companion left the hiding place. When he was discovered, he informed the searchers that he had been alone and hiding in another priest hole, which he showed them. He was then arrested and taken away.

A year later, the house was searched again. This time, Blount and his servant hid in a priest hole cut into the stone wall of a chamber, taking church vestments and books with them. They had to hide so quickly that Blount, who had been roused from his bed, wore only his breeches. With the householders locked away, the building was searched thoroughly for ten days with bricklayers and carpenters enlisted to help locate hiding places. During that time Blount and his companion had only a bottle of wine and a loaf of bread, but they managed to evade capture. Father Richard Blount, at least, survived, later becoming the head of the Jesuit English Mission.

ELIZABETH'S ALTAR CROSS

Although she was a Protestant, Elizabeth often displeased her more extreme subjects. She insisted that priests should wear vestments, putting her at odds with the more staunch English Protestants of the time. Similarly, her insistence that she keep candlesticks and a cross on the altar in the chapel royal was a major provocation. Many 16th-century Protestants were highly suspicious of any decoration in church, seeing it as idolatry. In 1562 and again in 1567, the cross and the candlesticks were removed without her permission, something which infuriated the queen. After 1567 she compromised by replacing the cross with a tapestry depicting the crucifixion, although this still caused objections.

THE SECRET SERVICE

Elizabeth I was ever-conscious of threats to her throne and employed spies to ensure that treason was reported to her when it arose. Her chief spymaster was Sir Francis Walsingham (1532–1590), who served as Elizabeth's principal secretary from 1573 until his death in 1590. Walsingham was a zealous Protestant and determined to find and root out Catholics in England. His networks stretched wide and it was he who devised the means to entrap Elizabeth's unwelcome guest, Mary, Queen of Scots, when she committed treason.

MARY, QUEEN OF SCOTS (1542–1588)

Mary, Queen of Scots succeeded to the throne of her native land when she was only six days old. Her father, James V, had been at war with England at the time of his death and conflicts continued for some years as Henry VIII attempted to gain control of his infant great-niece. Finally, the little queen was betrothed to the Dauphin of France and sent to be raised with him, with her husband succeeding to the French throne as Francis II in 1559. His reign lasted less than 18 months before his widow, the beautiful Mary, returned to Scotland to rule her kingdom personally for the first time.

Against Elizabeth's wishes, Mary married the English Henry Stuart, Lord Darnley (1545–1547), following her return to Scotland. Darnley was the son of Lady Margaret Douglas (1515–

1578), who was Mary's aunt and the woman with the second-best hereditary claim to the English crown. The marriage united the two claims, particularly with the birth, on 19 June 1566, of the couple's son, James.

Mary and Darnley's marriage was very unhappy, with "King" Henry proving to be a poor choice of husband. He was both jealous and unstable and, in March 1566, stabbed the queen's secretary to death as he clung to her skirts for protection.

A few months after Prince James's birth Mary, and the rest of Edinburgh, were awoken by a loud explosion. Upon investigation it was discovered that the house in which Darnley was staying had been blown up by gunpowder. Mary's husband was found dead in the orchard next to the house. He had been strangled.

When news of Darnley's death reached England, Elizabeth was uncomfortably reminded of the death of Amy Robsart. Her sympathies were with her fellow queen and she wrote, cautioning Mary on how she should be seen to behave. She stated "boldly" that she was "more sorrowful" for Mary than she was for her "killed cousin", Darnley, before continuing:

"O madam, I would not do the office of faithful cousin or affectionate friend if I studied rather to please your ears than employed myself in preserving your honour. However, I will not at all dissemble what most people are talking about: which is that you will look through your fingers at the revenging of this deed, and that you do not take measures that touch those who have done as you wished, as if the thing had been entrusted in a way that the murderers felt assurance in doing it. Among the thoughts in my heart I beseech you to want no such thought to stick at this point."

Mary, unfortunately, failed to heed Elizabeth's advice. On 15 May 1567 she married the Earl of Bothwell (1534–1578), who was widely regarded to be Darnley's murderer. A subsequent rebellion saw Mary imprisoned and deposed, with her infant son set upon the throne in her place. Elizabeth once again stood by her, refusing to recognize the new king and raging at the Scottish lords, but she offered no military assistance to her cousin. She was shocked when Mary, who managed to slip her guards, arrived unannounced in England on 17 May 1568.

Elizabeth promised her Catholic cousin her protection, but she refused to see her while she remained under suspicion of Darnley's murder. The pair never met, with the Queen of Scots remaining under house arrest far from London. Mary, not unnaturally, fiercely resented her captivity, and wrote to complain on occasion of her "sudden removal and change of keepers, and treatment of my servants" when she believed that the queen had promised to treat her more favourably. She ended, declaring that "I could only lament that my confidence in you and my friendship and desire to please you, have brought me a reward so unhoped for and evil, in reward for my loving forbearance". Mary, as a sister queen, particularly resented the fact that she had to request permission to even write to her cousin. She wanted Elizabeth to restore her to Scotland. At the same time, the Scottish queen was highly aware of her hereditary claim to England and had designs on Elizabeth's throne.

The presence of the woman many considered to be the heir to the throne was a major concern for Elizabeth. Mary's Catholicism made her the focus of plots, including one in 1571 which attempted to depose the queen and replace her with her Scottish cousin. This plot involved Thomas Howard, 4th Duke of Norfolk (1536–1572) – the premier peer in England and Elizabeth's cousin – who hoped to marry Mary and return the English church to Catholicism.

Norfolk was sentenced to death for his complicity, but the queen, who always baulked at ordering the deaths of her kin, hesitated. On 26 February 1571 she signed the warrant and dispatched it to the Tower, only to be "so greatly disquieted in mind and conscience that she could not rest until she had sent to the lieutenant to return it". She finally agreed to Norfolk's execution on 2 June 1572, but it caused her so much emotional turmoil that the Earl of Sussex was heard to comment that she needed a husband to keep her safe.

Mary continued to plot, both for her freedom and the English crown. In May 1586 a young Catholic gentleman called Anthony Babington (1561–1586) was contacted by one John Ballad (?–1586), a Catholic priest who had obtained Spanish support for a plot to murder Elizabeth. Babbington joined with Ballad and wrote to the Queen of Scots, asking her to support the enterprise. Unaware that Elizabeth's spies were reading the correspondence, Mary replied, agreeing to her cousin's murder.

This letter sealed Mary's fate. She was tried for treason in late 1586, accused of attempting to murder the queen. Mary, at first, refused to recognize the authority of the trial, declaring that "It seemeth strange to me, that the queen should command me as a subject to appear personally in judgment. I am an absolute queen". She appeared, nonetheless, complaining that she had arrived in England only to seek aid – something which had been refused. She denied all knowledge of Babbington or his plot, demanding that the court prove that she had received his letters. When shown her own letters, she burst into tears, declaring that "I would never make shipwreck of my soul by conspiring the destruction of my dearest sister".

Unsurprisingly, the Scottish queen was convicted, although, as with the Duke of Norfolk, Elizabeth was unwilling to sentence a family member to death. She prevaricated for several months, before signing the warrant and handing it to her secretary, William Davison (c.1541–1608). Taking the initiative before the queen could recall it, the warrant was dispatched to Fotheringhay Castle, where Mary was imprisoned. On 8 February 1588, Mary, Queen of Scots, who had spent nearly half her life in prison, stepped out into the great hall at Fotheringhay. Mary who in her youth had been tall and beautiful, still appeared imposing in her black satin gown and crimson petticoat. She prayed loudly in Latin before removing her outer gown. Kneeling at the block, she was beheaded with two strokes of the axe. Her lips stirred, as though in prayer, for quarter of an hour after she died.

The speedy execution solved a problem for Elizabeth. Regardless, she professed herself shocked when she heard the news and "her countenance altered, her speech faltered her, and through excessive sorrow she stood in a manner astonished". The queen was determined to find a scapegoat for an act that shocked much of Europe, writing to Mary's son to set out "how innocent I am in this case". She maintained that she had signed the warrant only for use in an emergency and that Davison had deliberately disobeyed her orders. At court, she raged at Davison, threatening to have him hanged. She eventually settled for his imprisonment.

Elizabeth's protestations of guilt were highly convenient and the fact remains that she did sign the death warrant. The scapegoating of Davison was enough, however, to ensure continuing friendship with Scotland, particularly since James VI had hopes of being named as Elizabeth's heir. Not all foreign rulers were so content. Philip of Spain had begun building an invasion fleet even before Mary's "martyrdom". He intended to conquer England and return it to the Catholic faith.

13

WAR AND DISCOVERY

After turning down Philip of Spain's early marriage offer, relations between Elizabeth and her brother-in-law began to sour. The pair clashed on nearly every aspect of their policies and it was Philip's response, the Spanish Armada of 1588, which provided the highpoint of the Tudor queen's long reign.

SIR FRANCIS DRAKE (C.1540–1596)

When invasion threatened, Elizabeth had a number of well-qualified men to assist in the defence of her kingdom. The hero of the Spanish Armada was a very experienced sailor by 1588. Francis Drake, a native of Devon, made his first journey to the Americas in the 1560s in the company of his cousin, Sir John Hawkins.

He became famous when, in 1577, he set out to circumnavigate the world in his ship, the *Golden Hind*, a voyage that would take him three years. He headed south at first, along the coast of West Africa, before crossing the Atlantic and moving around the shores of South America. He reached California, which he claimed for England, before daringly crossing the Pacific. He then made his way towards Indonesia before sailing around the tip of Africa and making his way home. During the voyage Drake, who was effectively a state-sponsored pirate, attacked the Spanish colonies and robbed their ships of gold. To the queen's delight, he came home with his ship filled with Spanish treasure.

The voyage of the *Golden Hind* was one of the most daring in an age of exploration. Drake continued his seafaring ways until his death from dysentery in Panama in 1596.

THE SPANISH ARMADA

Philip II of Spain was infuriated by the queen's Protestantism, as well as her foreign policy in which she aided his rebellious subjects in the Netherlands. English piracy against Spanish shipping also did not help matters. Although Philip claimed the credit for bringing the queen to the throne, this was something that Elizabeth disputed.

Philip began to prepare for military action early in 1586. Word of this quickly reached England and, in April 1587, Francis Drake set fire to the ships in Cadiz harbour, thus "Singeing the beard of the king of Spain". The raid, which destroyed around 100 ships, delayed the invasion by a year.

In May 1588, 130 Spanish ships containing 20,000 armed men set sail from Lisbon bound for England. Owing to bad weather, it almost immediately had to return to port, only sailing again on 12 July. Aware of the threat, Elizabeth had placed her cousin, Lord Howard of Effingham, and the sailor, Francis Drake, in command of her fleet, with the men under orders to intercept the Armada before it could land in England.

The Armada made slow progress but, finally, on 19 July, it was sighted off Cornwall, heading into the English Channel. Warning beacons were immediately lit along the south coast, providing an efficient means of conveying the news quickly. According to legend, Drake was playing bowls on Plymouth Hoe when the fleet was sighted, showing a calm and cool-headed demeanour as he insisted first on finishing his game. Drake and Howard had already assembled a large fleet and they sailed into the Channel to engage the Spanish as soon as the weather permitted. These encounters proved to be ineffective and the Spanish fleet was able to anchor off Calais, waiting for further troops to arrive from the Netherlands.

This inactivity gave the English a chance to save the situation. Drake sent five unmanned and burning ships into the Armada fleet in the night, causing panic as the Spaniards struggled to cut their anchors and sail out to sea to escape the flames. On 29 July they were attacked by the English again and, this time, the already weakened Armada was scattered, with the remnant of the fleet being chased as far north as the Firth of Forth. Very few survivors made it home to Spain and the Armada proved to be the most decisive military victory of the Tudor dynasty.

ELIZABETH I AT TILBURY

The Armada was only intended to be the fleet that conveyed troops to England. The invasion itself would be fought on English soil. The Armada troops numbered nearly 20,000. They were divided into 162 companies and armed to the hilt with firearms and fearsome pikes, making a formidable host. Elizabeth placed her beloved Robert Dudley, who had recently returned from fighting in the Netherlands, at the head of her army, trusting him to defend her kingdom. He mustered his troops at Tilbury in Essex in late July 1588, raising around 12,500 men, while another 6,000 troops were waiting at Sandwich. Troops were also expected from other parts of the country.

It took news of the Armada's ultimate defeat some time to reach Elizabeth and she was still unaware that the danger had entirely passed on 9 August 1588 when she set out to review her troops at Tilbury. Dressed in a silver breastplate over a white dress, she appeared Amazonian. Elizabeth made the most famous speech of her reign, declaring that "I know I have the body but of a weak and feeble woman, but I have the heart and stomach of a king and of a king of England too – and take foul scorn that Parma [the Armada's commander] or any other prince of Europe should dare to invade the borders of my realm".

When she heard the news of the Armada's defeat, Elizabeth was overjoyed, ordering public thanksgiving across England, as well as personally going in procession through London in a chariot. For Elizabeth, the celebrations of the greatest triumph of her reign ended abruptly on 4 September 1588 when Robert Dudley died.

DUDLEY'S LAST LETTER

When Elizabeth received word of Dudley's death, she shut herself in her chamber, refusing to come out. Finally, her council ordered that the door be broken open. Even then, Elizabeth still refused to conduct business for some time, referring to Dudley in a letter of the time as a "personage so dear to us". Shortly before his death,

Dudley had written to the queen, asking her about her health and trying to assuage her worries about his own illness. When Elizabeth's papers were examined after her own death, this letter was found, inscribed in her own hand with the words "His last letter". The loss of her adored favourite aged Elizabeth, although she still had nearly 15 years left to live.

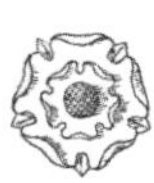

THE ENGLISH NAVY

Victory over the Armada had only been made possible thanks to the actions of the queen's father earlier in the 16th century. Henry VIII was proud of his navy, building it up from almost nothing during his reign. He began to create a permanent fleet in 1514. Tudor battleships were large and unwieldy – like small floating castles. Although they had guns, they were designed for hand-to-hand combat, with two ships being grappled together so that their crews could engage.

Henry VIII's greatest ship had been the *Mary Rose*, which was built in 1510. A vast ship, it weighed 600 tonnes and had room for around 500 men. All three of its decks held cannons, which were fired through gun ports, although personal combat was still important, with the ship holding weapons, such as bows.

The *Mary Rose* sank in 1545 in Portsmouth Harbour during an attack by a French invasion fleet. It had around 400 people aboard, of which only a handful survived, as the horrified king watched from the shore. It is still not certain what caused the ship to sink. One eyewitness claimed that it was turning after it had fired the guns on one side, something that caused the water to enter the gun ports. Other theories are that it was caught by a gust of wind or struck by French cannonballs. Whatever occurred, Henry VIII's great flagship was raised from the Solent in 1982 and can be visited at Portsmouth.

Elizabeth followed her father in maintaining a standing navy. When Henry VIII died, he had a fleet of 53 ships, although his successors maintained a navy of only around half this number. As well as keeping a standing navy, the last Tudor queen was also interested in seafaring because of the possibilities it opened up for adventure, colonization and trade.

ROANOKE ISLAND

Sir Francis Drake was not the only one of Elizabeth's subjects to venture to the New World. The Americas, which had first been "discovered" by Europeans in 1492, fascinated the Tudors. While South America was largely claimed by the time of Elizabeth's accession, much of North America was still available.

The queen's dashing favourite, Sir Walter Raleigh (1552–1618), set out in 1584 with the aim of creating a colony in North America. He decided upon Roanoake Island, which is in modern North Carolina. When the expedition returned to England, they brought two Native Americans with them, Manteo and Wanchese. The two men caused a sensation at court, with Manteo, in particular, learning English and providing his hosts with information about his homeland and way of life.

The following year, Manteo and Wanchese returned to Roanoke in a small fleet carrying more than 100 colonists. The first colony was quickly abandoned because of difficulties in getting supplies from England. New colonists arrived in 1587, creating a more permanent settlement. The colonists built a fort and homes and began to grow crops; Virginia Dare became the first English child to be born in the New World.

All seemed well at Roanoake but, when English ships returned with supplies in 1590, they found it abandoned. Nothing was heard of the first colonists again and the mystery of their disappearance was never solved. It was, however, to be the first of many colonies in North America, with the English establishing a lasting presence there.

NEW FOODS AND FADS

The discovery of the New World profoundly changed people's diets. The potato was reportedly introduced by Sir Thomas Harriot (c.1560–1621) in 1586, although it was widely believed to be poisonous and was still not regularly eaten a century later. Tomatoes had arrived in England a little earlier, although they were also not eaten by most people for some years. Tobacco, on the other hand, proved rather more popular when it was introduced from the New World. It was smoked in pipes from the 1570s and, unlike the suspicious potato and tomato, was believed to have health benefits. Not everyone approved of smoking, however. James VI (1566–1625) of Scotland loathed it.

Other foods familiar in Europe today had their origins in the Americas. Pumpkins, sweetcorn and chilli peppers came from there, as did turkeys.

JAPAN

English explorers did not only visit the New World. An Englishman, William Adams (1564–1620), sailed with the Dutch to south-east Asia in 1598. He became the first English visitor to Japan in 1600, remaining there until his death in 1620. He was held in high regard there, involving himself in trade as well as marrying and starting a family. His knowledge of sailing was in particular demand with the Japanese.

14

GLORIANA

Elizabeth always insisted that "So long as I live, I shall be queen of England; when I am dead, they shall succeed that has most right". As she aged, she faced many challenges to her rule and authority, but she weathered these storms, outliving any other Tudor monarch. She was the last, and the greatest.

MALE FAVOURITES

Elizabeth continued to attract suitors up to the end of her life. One of her most devoted was Sir Christopher Hatton (1540–1591), who always remained single as a result of his love for the queen. In recompense, Elizabeth grieved sincerely for him when he died in November 1591. When Sir Walter Raleigh, arrived at court in 1581 he immediately attracted the queen's attention. He was tall, handsome and only in his late 20s. The couple flirted at court although, in the autumn of 1591, Raleigh secretly married one of the queen's ladies. Elizabeth could never bear it when her favourites married and, when she discovered what had happened the following year, she placed her erstwhile favourite under house arrest.

THE EARL OF ESSEX (1565–1601)

Elizabeth's last favourite was the handsome Robert Devereux, Earl of Essex who, as a great-grandson of Mary Boleyn was also the queen's distant cousin. The young man, who was more than 30 years Elizabeth's junior, first arrived at court in the 1580s in the company of his stepfather, Robert Dudley (c.1532–1588). He immediately caught the queen's eye, being both young and handsome. In her affection, she was able to ignore the fact that he was also vain, arrogant and ambitious. Dismissing these faults, Elizabeth placed him in command of her army in Ireland.

Safe in the knowledge of Elizabeth's indulgent affection, as the years went by, Essex's behaviour became increasingly outrageous. On 28 September 1598, the earl, having returned to England from Ireland without the queen's permission, burst into her chamber while she was dressing. His intrusion debunked the myth that she had been untouched by time and he saw her without cosmetics or her elaborate wigs – a wrinkled old woman with thin grey hair. In spite of her fury and embarrassment, Elizabeth kept her composure and had a private interview with Essex, but she was never able to forgive him for shattering the illusion that she had carefully built.

Essex continued to consider himself untouchable, gathering a party of disaffected men around him, including his new stepfather, the Catholic Sir Christopher Blount (c.1555–1601). Together with his followers, Essex conceived a plot to imprison Elizabeth so that he could rule in her place as Lord Protector. On 8 February 1601, Essex imprisoned some of the queen's council members in his house before setting out into London with 150 armed followers. He had always been popular and hoped to gain support from the people of the city. In this he was to be disappointed. Although Elizabeth's popularity waned in the last decade of her life, the people were not prepared to join with Essex. Unable to attract any support, he returned to his house to consider his next move.

Elizabeth was informed immediately of Essex's action and reacted furiously, threatening to "have gone out in person to see what any rebel of them all durst do against her". She refused to sleep until Essex and his supporters had been arrested, ordering cannon to be brought from the Tower to force him from his house. It was the threat that his house would be blown up that persuaded the fallen favourite to give himself up, and the earl was taken at once to the Tower. His rebellion was a futile and short-lived affair and the queen showed him no mercy, ordering his execution on 25 February 1601. The Earl of Essex was to be Elizabeth's last favourite.

WILLIAM SHAKESPEARE (1564–1616) AND THE ELIZABETHAN THEATRE

The theatre was one of the greatest attractions in Elizabethan London, thanks to a number of talented playwrights active in the period. By far the most successful was William Shakespeare, the son of a glovemaker from Stratford-upon-Avon, who was born in 1564.

Shakespeare, who began his career as an actor, soon became famous for the plays he composed from the 1590s onwards. As well as classics such as *Romeo and Juliet*, *Hamlet*, *Othello* and *Macbeth*, he wrote lesser known dramas, such as *Titus Andronicus* and *A Comedy of Errors*. Shakespeare's works – tragedies, histories and comedies – spanned the genres, and he was by far the most popular dramatist of his day.

Along with his business partners, he built The Globe Theatre in London, which was the leading playhouse until it burned to the ground during a performance of Shakespeare's *Henry VIII* in 1613. A replica of the Globe was rebuilt in the 1990s and performances, which can be enjoyed from wooden benches or standing in front of the stage, can be watched today.

WHO WROTE SHAKESPEARE'S PLAYS?

William Shakespeare came from an unlikely background for a playwright, something that has led to the authorship of the works of the man who the dramatist Robert Greene (1558–1592) described as an "upstart crow" to be challenged. Instead, the Earl of Oxford, Sir Francis Bacon (1561–1626) or the unfortunate dramatist, Christopher Marlowe (1564–1693), who died in a tavern brawl, have been posited as the true author. Other, more farcical, suggestions have included Elizabeth I herself.

In all cases, it is argued that the true author was a prominent figure, who wished to be a playwright, and was forced to write under a pseudonym. In order to publish, they used the identity of an obscure actor from Stratford-upon-Avon as the public face of their work. The controversy will probably never die away, although William Shakespeare, the genius son of a glovemaker must be the most likely author of "Shakespeare's" plays.

FLUSHING THE TOILET

As well as developments in the arts, the Elizabethan period saw more practical developments. Although childless herself, Elizabeth stood as godmother to many children, including Sir John Harrington (1561–1612). Harrington holds distinction as the inventor of the flushing toilet – a practical and hygienic innovation that would not become commonplace for 400 years.

While living at his house at Kelston, Harrington designed and installed the world's first flushing lavatory, which was named an "Ajax". He was so pleased with his invention, which involved a complicated system of weights and levers to open a valve beneath a pan, that he showed it to his godmother when she visited in 1592. Legend has it that the queen tested the device, giving it her approval, although it failed to catch on.

THE GOLDEN SPEECH

By the early 1600s Elizabeth was in her late 60s and her health was failing. Few expected her to live for much longer and there was a sense in England of the ending of an era. She had already reigned for more than 40 years when, on 30 November 1601, she set out to address Parliament for what would be the last time, making a speech that would be considered to be her "Golden Speech".

As she spoke, Elizabeth set out her affection for her people, declaring "There will never queen sit in my seat with more zeal to my country, care to my subjects, and that will soon with willingness venture her life for your good and safety, than myself". She had always considered that she had been brought to the throne through the love of the people and that she represented them, adding that "It is not my desire to live nor reign longer than my life and reign shall be for your good. And though you have had and may have many princes more mighty and wise sitting in this seat, yet you never had or shall have any that will be more careful and loving". It was Elizabeth's swan song.

THE SUCCESSION

Elizabeth always refused to name her successor for fear that they would attract a party around them, as she had done during her sister's reign. By 1600, there were a number of rival candidates, each of whom hoped to take the crown.

By strict hereditary rank, the heir to the throne was James VI of Scotland (1566–1625), who was twice a great-grandson of Henry VIII's elder sister, Margaret Tudor. His mother, Mary, Queen of Scots, was Margaret's granddaughter – the only child of the Tudor princess's only son. Margaret also had another surviving child, Lady Margaret Douglas, who was the mother of James VI's father, Henry, Lord Darnley. Her younger son, Charles Stuart, had also produced a child – Arbella Stuart – who was raised in England and also considered a possible heir to the throne.

Under the terms of Henry VIII's will, the legal heirs to the throne were the descendants of his sister, Mary. She had two daughters: Frances and Eleanor Brandon. Of Frances's children, only Catherine Grey produced issue. Her elder son, Edward Seymour, Lord Beauchamp, had impressed the queen when he visited her at court in June 1582, reading from a Latin book at her request. In spite of his "illegitimacy", he was a leading contender for the throne, particularly since, by 1602, he was already the father of three sons. While an anonymous letter from the period said that Lord Beauchamp or Arbella Stuart might be "fit enough to make a Queen Jane [Grey] of", by 1603 it was almost universally understood that the next monarch would be James of Scotland.

ARBELLA STUART (1575–1615)

Arbella Stuart, who was a great-granddaughter of Henry VII, had the best hereditary claim to the throne after James of Scotland and his children. She was raised and educated under the governorship of her maternal grandmother, the famous Bess of Hardwick, Countess of Shrewsbury. The marriage of her parents, Charles Stuart and Elizabeth Cavendish had infuriated the queen, with the groom's mother, the royal Lady Margaret Douglas, sent to the Tower. Arbella was orphaned in her early childhood and spent time with her aunt, Mary, Queen of Scots, whose gaoler was her step-grandfather, the Earl of Shrewsbury.

Arbella was raised to be highly aware of her proximity to the throne, although Elizabeth tended to ignore her, as she had done the Grey sisters. The relationship between the queen and her cousin was so poor that, when Arbella was asked to act as chief mourner at Elizabeth's funeral, she refused, saying "that since her access to the queen in her lifetime might not be permitted, she would not after her death be brought upon the stage for a public spectacle".

Her attempts to arrange a marriage with Catherine Grey's grandson in 1602 may well have been a bid for the crown. Certainly, this was how James I viewed her secret marriage to William Seymour (1588–1660) (another of Catherine Grey's grandsons) in 1610. Both were imprisoned, although Seymour managed to escape to France. His wife died in the Tower in 1615.

FLOCKING TO THE NEW MONARCH

The diaries of Lady Anne Clifford, who was a child in 1603, show that Elizabeth was correct to worry about people flocking to the new monarch. Immediately following Elizabeth's funeral, noblewomen and gentlewomen flocked to meet the new king's wife, Anne of Denmark (1574–1619), as she moved south from Scotland. Everyone wanted to be the first to greet the new queen and secure her favour or a coveted place in her household. Lady Anne Clifford and her mother were no exception, killing three horses during their fast ride northwards. Although not the first to greet the new queen, they did gain some preferment from her, being regularly in her company when the court was staying at Basingstoke following the new king and queen's coronation.

THE DEATH OF ELIZABETH TUDOR

The Tudor dynasty – personified by Elizabeth – must have seemed endless. By 1603 many in England could not remember a time when she had not been queen. Certainly, no one could recall a time before her father, Henry VIII, sat on the throne. The Tudor dynasty seemed mighty and secure, but its end was approaching as the queen aged. Not long before her death, Elizabeth's coronation ring, which she never removed, had to be filed off when it was discovered that it had grown into the flesh of her finger. It was taken by many, said William Camden, as an ill omen, "as if it portended that her marriage with the kingdom, contracted with that Ring, would now be dissolved".

Early in 1603 Elizabeth suffered from a sore throat, causing it to swell and making breathing difficult. She was 69 years old – ancient for the times – and depressed about the death of her friend, the Countess of Nottingham. She refused, at first, to come to bed in her illness, instead sitting on cushions on the floor, sucking her finger and staring blankly. She finally consented to enter her bed on 22 March after being implored for several days by her ministers and ladies. Legend has it that, as she lay dying, she was asked about her successor, and gaspingly replied: "I said that my throne was the throne of kings, that I would not have any mean person succeed me", before naming the King of Scots. More likely, Elizabeth died as she had lived, resolutely refusing to name an heir for fear that those around her would rush towards them and abandon her.

Elizabeth I died on 24 March 1603. The Tudor dynasty, which had endured for three generation and for nearly 120 years died with her. Unlike other dynastic changes, the path from the Tudors to their successors, the Stuarts, was peaceful. By living so long and surviving most of the major claimants, the childless Elizabeth had provided for the succession after all. James VI of Scotland, the first Stuart king of England, was the only logical successor.

FURTHER READING

Numerous books have been written on the Tudors. Those listed below provide an excellent introduction to the dynasty, as well as the fascinating people, innovations and discoveries of the age.

There are many biographies of the Tudor monarchs, with the earliest dating to the 16th and 17th centuries. For Henry VII, try Chrimes, S B, *Henry VII* (Yale, 1999) and Penn, T, *Winter King* (London, 2012) for a detailed account of his life. Henry VIII is, perhaps, the most written about Tudor, with several biographies, including Loades, D, *Henry VIII* (Stroud, 2011) and Wooding, L, *Henry VIII* (London, 2008). A highly readable account of Edward VI is Skidmore, C, *Edward VI: The Lost King of England* (London, 2008). For Mary Tudor, there is Porter, L, *Mary Tudor: The First Queen* (London, 2009) and Prescott, H F M, *Mary Tudor: The Spanish Tudor* (London, 2003). By far the most detailed account of Elizabeth is Somerset, A, *Elizabeth I* (London, 2002).

Henry VIII's six wives also continue to fascinate. For group biographies of all six wives, try Fraser, A, *The Six Wives of Henry VIII* (London, 2009), Starkey, D, *Six Wives* (London, 2004) and Weir, A, *The Six Wives of Henry VIII* (London, 2007). Each wife has also been the subject of at least one individual biography. Tremlett, G, *Catherine of Aragon* (London, 2011) is an excellent recent account of Henry VIII's first wife. For Anne Boleyn, the most detailed is Ives, E, *The Life and Death of Anne Boleyn* (London, 2005), while Norton, E, *The Anne Boleyn Papers* (Stroud, 2013) includes most of the original sources relating to Henry VIII's second wife. For Henry's final four wives, consider Loades, D, *Jane Seymour* (Stroud, 2013), Norton, E, *Jane Seymour: Henry VIII's True Love* (Stroud, 2009), Norton, E, *Anne of Cleves: Henry VIII's Discarded Bride* (Stroud, 2009), Smith, L B, *Catherine Howard* (Stroud, 2010), James, S, *Catherine Parr: Henry VIII's Last Love* (Stroud, 2008) and Norton, E, *Catherine Parr* (Stroud, 2010)

There have been many biographies of prominent Tudor figures, including these: Fraser, A, *Mary Queen of Scots* (London, 2009), Gristwood, S, *Arbella: England's Lost Queen* (London, 2004), Gristwood, S, *Elizabeth and Leicester* (London, 2008), Hutchinson, R, *Thomas Cromwell* (London, 2009), Lisle, L, de, *The Sisters Who Would Be Queen* (London, 2009), MacCulloch, D, *Thomas Cranmer* (Yale, 1997), Norton, E, *Margaret Beaufort* (Stroud, 2010) and Shapiro, J, 1599: *A Year in the Life of William Shakespeare* (London, 2006)

For the Tudor government and religion, Bernard, G W, *The King's Reformation* (Yale, 2007), Haynes, A, *Invisible Power: The Elizabethan Secret Services* (Stroud, 1992), Duffy, E, *The Stripping of the Altars* (Yale, 2005) and Duffy, E, *Fires of the Faith: Catholic England Under Mary Tudor* (Yale, 2010) are very detailed.

Tudor daily life is recorded in a wide variety of sources. You can read more in Mortimer, I, *The Time Traveller's Guide to Elizabethan England* (London, 2013) and Sim, A, *Food and Feast in Tudor England* (Stroud, 2005)

Finally, for science, discovery and warfare, Hart-Davis, A, *What the Tudors & Stuarts Did For Us* (London, 2002), Martin, C and Parker, G, *The Spanish Armada* (London, 1988) and Milton, G, *Big Chief Elizabeth* (London, 2001) are very readable and give detailed accounts.